# **Puppy** Training

# Puppy Training

## The Essential Guide for all Puppy Owners

### DAVID SQUIRE & PATRICIA KING

APPLE

First published in the UK in 2012 by
**Apple Press**
7 Greenland Street
London NW1 0ND
United Kingdom
www.apple-press.com

ISBN 978-1-84543-445-8

1 3 5 7 9 10 8 6 4 2

PRODUCED BY
**Fine Folio Publishing Limited**
6 Bourne Terrace, Bourne Hill, Wherstead, Ipswich, Suffolk, IP2 8NG, UK

DESIGNER
Glyn Bridgewater

ILLUSTRATOR
Coral Mula

EDITOR
Alison Copland

Printed in China by Voion.

# Contents

# Introduction

If that wolf nestling by your hearth appears to be winking at you, it is because he knows he is 'on to a winner'. Regular meals, warmth and adoration are his for the asking – he has certainly come a long way from roughing it in a forest and pursuing his own food. Yet he has played his part in this evolution – offering in return protection, companionship and unreserved affection.

*Many dogs delight in leaping and bounding through snow.*

Who gets more out of this symbiotic relationship is debatable, but certainly today's domestic dogs are more successful than they would have been if still roaming in a cold forest. Their numbers are greater and their survival more certain. And that is evolution at its best.

For man, dogs have evolved and been selectively bred to assist in many of his endeavours, from hunting and herding to drawing carts and sledges, aiding security forces in detection work, killing rats and searching for truffles. Surprisingly, too, they are able to sniff and detect diseases in their owners, often before symptoms are developed.

Increasingly, dogs act as guides and assistance animals for people who have sight, hearing and mobility problems. There can also be no doubt about the ways in which dogs have gained our affection with their sensitive interactions in times of personal anxiety and stress, often becoming incomparable confidants.

Puppies need guidance if they are to achieve successful relationships with us and their lives are to become interwoven with our own. This book comprehensively explains the initial training of a puppy and, later, when an adult.

If you love dogs and you want one of them to become part of your life – whether within a family or solely as a companion animal – this book offers detailed guidance.

*Mother and puppy of the Alaskan Malamute, a hardy and remarkably strong northern sledge breed.*

# THE HEALTHY PUPPY AND DOG

# Signs of good health

When buying a puppy or dog – from whatever the source – it is essential to choose a healthy, well-formed animal with a lively and friendly disposition. There is often an inclination to take pity on the weakest and most dejected animal in a litter and to buy that one, but this is a mistake as it may never develop into a healthy dog which becomes a reliable member of your family. Also, it may also prove to be physically weak and susceptible to long-term medical problems, which can be financially costly to treat.

Some indications of a healthy puppy or dog are easily seen, but if you are in any doubt about the animal's health you must consult a vet.

Here are some of the signs of good health:

● **Abdomen**: This should be slightly rounded, but not bulging and excessively protruding. It should be soft and flexible, not pot-bellied and stretched like a drum. Check there is no swelling around the navel.

*There is a close rapport between a mother and her puppy.*

In puppies, tummies are often slightly swollen and this reduces with age, exercise and natural development.

● **Anus**: The orifice through which excrement is expelled. This – and the area around it – should be clean and without any sign of staining; neither should there be matting or dried faeces.

Incidentally, puppies and dogs are likely to sniff at each others' anal area; this is quite natural as they distinguish and identify their companions by smells arising from that area.

● **Action**: Puppies have their own and distinctive movement, often short bursts of activity, then long rests. Remember that a young puppy may sleep for 16 out of 24 hours. Puppies tend to gamble and may, when excited, fall over their own feet, but there should be no sign of lameness or limping.

● **Appetite**: There should be a general interest in food, but not with an excessively ravenous nature. Keenness to eat varies from one breed to another and large breeds normally eat faster than miniature types. Check the puppy's mouth area for signs of vomiting after eating too much food.

● **Attitude**: A quick and alert response to sound and movement is essential, with a curious nature, vitality and questioning attitude indicating intelligence.

*Throughout puppyhood, regularly check for healthy growth. All limbs should move freely.*

• **Breathing**: Must be even and not laboured, especially when the animal is quiet and resting. In summer, the animal might be panting in order to keep cool, but this is natural. However, there certainly must not be any sign or sound of coughing or croaking and a straining of the throat muscles.

• **Claws**: Lift up each paw to check that the foot is intact and the claws have not split. They should not be excessively long or overgrown.

• **Coat**: Must be clean and free from loose hairs and engrained dirt. If you run you hand over it the texture should be soft. Additionally, it must have a pleasant smell – not 'stale' or excessively 'doggy'.

• **Ears**: No sign of scratching and rubbing, and the animal not shaking its head and ears. The ears should be alert and held in their normal position, ready to hear the slightest sound. Check that they are not covered in yellow or brown deposits.

• **Eyes**: These reveal the sparkle and soul of a puppy and must be clear, showing no cloudiness of the cornea or general discharge, weeping or being bloodshot. Additionally, they should not be unduly sensitive to light.

• **Foot pads**: Essentially, they should be clean and not cracked, without matting of hair between them. Incidentally, thoroughly wash the pads in warm water if contaminated by salt used as a de-icing agent on paths and roads.

● **Faeces**: These are usually passed out of the animal two, three or four times each day; they vary in colour according to the diet. Check if they are evenly formed and with no sign of diarrhoea. Consult a vet if there is continuing diarrhoea.

● **Noses**: There should be no discharge, and neither nostril blocked with mucus (dried or runny). The external appearance of the nose varies: if the animal is out of doors, it will be cold and damp; when indoors, it will be warm and dry.

● **Skin**: Essentially, it should be clean and free from sores and parasites. As you run your hand over the coat, the skin must be supple and loose.

● **Teeth**: Puppies naturally shed their milk teeth, but adult ones should be clean and white, with gums pink. However, those of the Chow Chow may reveal darker shades. Be aware that puppies, when teething, may be prone to fits. Should this happen, immediately contact a vet.

● **Urine**: Both dogs and bitches should be able to pass urine frequently, freely and with no difficulty. It should be straw-coloured and not cloudy; there must be no sign of blood. Incidentally, until puberty puppies of both sexes tend to squat while passing urine. Then, females continue to squat while males revert to 'cocking a leg'. However, it has been known for dogs to squat throughout their lives.

*Long-haired Dachshund puppies have inquisitive and questioning expressions.*

## Keeping your puppy and dog healthy

Once established in your home your puppy – then dog – will be with you for eight or more years. During this time, he will get to know you well and be totally reliant on you for his welfare. Here are some of his needs for continuing well-being:

★ **Healthy and regular food**: The food required by a puppy or dog is described in the chapter on 'Feeding puppies and dogs', page 136.

★ **Regular exercise**: Together with a healthy diet, daily walks and play times in parks and fields are the ways to keep your pet healthy and trim. Training your dog to walk on a lead and to be obedient is essential, and this is described in the chapter on 'Puppy and dog training', page 96.

★ **Clean bedding and living area**: Making your puppy or dog comfortable during the day and at night is essential, and this is described in the chapter on 'Introducing a puppy to your home', page 86.

★ **Pest and disease free**: Regular checks for parasites and diseases are essential and many problems become apparent when grooming and stroking your puppy or dog. These are described fully in the chapter on 'Dealing with medical and other problems', page 146.

★ **... and last, but certainly not least, love and affection**: Dogs are pack animals and need to feel welcome and comfortable with you and your family. A happy dog is a pleasure to have next to you and will live longer than one which is neglected and feels unwanted.

*All puppies should have an alert nature.*

# What makes up a dog?

When reading books about dogs, talking with a veterinary surgeon or discussing dogs with friends, some of the following features of a dog's body might be mentioned.

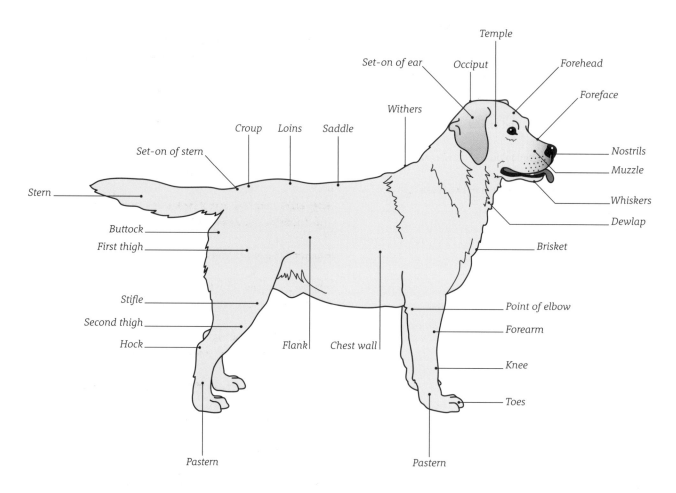

*Sizes and shapes of dogs vary from one breed to another, but here are the main features.*

**Points of a dog** (the descriptions below are in clockwise rotation, starting from the top right of the illustration on page 14)

★ **Forehead**: Area on the face between the eyes and ears.

★ **Foreface**: The front part of the head; between the nose and the eyes.

★ **Nostrils**: Orifices through which air is inhaled and expelled. With some breeds, breathing has become restricted.

★ **Muzzle**: The head in front of the eyes – nasal bone, nostrils and jaw.

★ **Whiskers**: On the face and especially on the chin.

★ **Dewlap**: Loose and pendulous skin under the throat.

★ **Brisket**: The part of the body in front of the chest and between the forelegs.

★ **Point of elbow**: The joint between the upper arm and the forearm.

★ **Forearm**: The bone of the foreleg between the elbow and the pastern.

★ **Knee**: The jointed area on a leg.

★ **Toes**: The bottom area on a foot, with pads and toenails.

★ **Pastern**: The lowest part of the leg; below the knee on the foreleg or below the hock on the hind leg.

★ **Chest wall**: Area just behind the chest.

★ **Flank**: The side of the body between the last rib and the hip.

★ **Hock**: The joint of the rear leg, analogous to the ankle in humans.

★ **Second thigh**: The lower part of the thigh, below the stifle.

★ **Stifle**: The joint of a hind leg, between the first thigh and the second thigh. It is analogous to the knee in humans.

★ **First thigh**: The upper part of the thigh, above the stifle.

★ **Buttock**: The 'bottom' area.

★ **Stern**: Often used to refer to the tail area.

★ **Set-on of stern**: The part of the hindquarters where the root of the tail is set into the body.

★ **Croup**: The rear part of the back, above the hind legs.

★ **Loins**: The region of the body on either side of the backbone and between the last ribs and the hindquarters.

★ **Saddle**: A black marking over the back, resembling a saddle. This marking, of course, is not seen in all breeds.

★ **Withers**: The highest part of the body, just behind the neck.

★ **Set-on of ear**: The angle at which the ears rest on the face.

★ **Occiput**: The upper, back point of the skull.

★ **Temple**: The area behind the eyes and below the ears.

# CHOOSING A PUPPY OR DOG

# What you need to consider

Choosing a puppy can be one of the most magical times in the life of a family. Even just talking about the prospect of an animal sharing your life is a joy and something to be cherished. Like all major family changes, however, it must be planned and undertaken only after thorough consideration for the animal and how it will integrate into your life. As the Dogs Trust's adage correctly suggests, 'a dog is for life, not just for Christmas', and this could, perhaps, encompass ten or more years into the future. Dogs Trust, by the way, is a leading animal welfare society for puppies and dogs.

## The whys and wherefores of having a puppy

This chapter unveils the many considerations when selecting a puppy – or adult animal – and encouraging it to be a successful part of your family. Having a puppy is full of fun, but it also brings about responsibilities.

This puppy-keeping checklist guides you through the essential questions of having a puppy, or dog, in your life.

## How much will it cost?

This is variable, and in addition to the initial buying there are food and medical costs throughout the animal's life.

● **Cost of buying a puppy or adult animal**: Always buy a puppy or dog through a reliable source, not out of the back of a car or from an entry on the internet.

The cost of buying a puppy varies depending on the source, whether from animal welfare societies or reputable breeders. Local vets often know of puppies that need good homes and this can be inexpensive, especially if the puppy's owners want to be assured that one of their bitch's puppies is 'going to a good home'.

Good ways of sourcing puppies are detailed on pages 24–27.

● **Injections and medical care**: Apart from a puppy's initial vaccinations, which are usually arranged by the bitch's owners, there will always be continuing expenses for medical care. Pet insurance plans are popular, but always check with the small print to ensure you will be 'getting what you expect', perhaps several years into the future. Allow for premiums to increase as your dog becomes older.

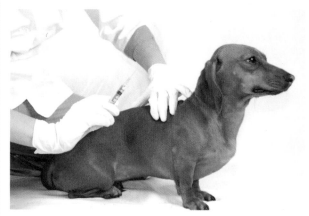

*Vaccinations are essential for the long-term health and well-being of both puppies and dogs.*

• **Cost of keeping a puppy**: Clearly, this is influenced by the breed and its eventual size. Puppies and dogs must be fed 'good' food every day – not just scraps of food occasionally given to them. They will also need dog biscuits and, invariably, 'treats'.

• **Microchipping**: This is a way of implanting ownership details into your dog to ensure that if he wanders off there is a good chance of him being recovered. The chip number allocated to the animal is recorded on a database. Costs vary but are not too high and well worth the expense as the emotional stress of losing a treasured pet is immense.

*Make sure water bowls for puppies are secure: this is a shallow metal dish, others are heavier and pottery-based.*

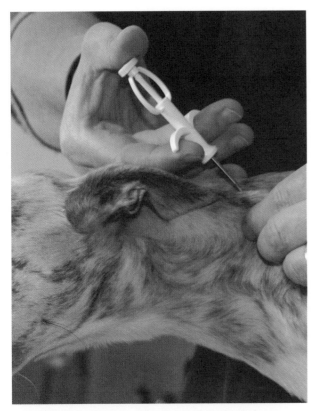

*Microchipping a dog is a painless procedure that helps to safeguard the animal throughout its life.*

• **Cost of equipment**: Food and water bowls are essential, together with leads, baskets and a dog blanket to make it more comfortable for him.

## A matter of choice

• **Puppy or dog?**: Many families like to start with a puppy, especially if their family is young. But rehousing an older dog can be just as fulfilling, with the benefit of the animal usually being house-trained. Each of these needs special attention to help them settle into family life; for a puppy these are described on pages 88–95, and for a rescued dog on page 25). Rescued dogs often become superb family pets.

• **Male or female?**: Whether a bitch or dog is most suitable as a family pet is a perennial question. There are differing views about the choice and some families have a tradition of keeping a bitch, others a dog. Nevertheless, whatever the decision, there is always the possibility of neutering the animal (see below).

Most people would agree that a bitch is more home-loving and less tempted to roam than a dog, but an element of this waywardness is the result of bad training. A dog which is not allowed to roam the streets and is given a comfortable home life, together with strict supervision and training when young, will not give you any problems.

*Puppies and dogs quickly respond to affection, a comfortable home and the correct diet for their age.*

The major difficulty with a bitch is to keep her at home and away from dogs when she is in season (a time when she could become pregnant if mated).

If you have concerns about a bitch getting out when in season and mating inappropriately, then the answer is to have her spayed. It would be irresponsible to risk bringing unwanted puppies into your home, with all its attendant expenses and difficulties, not the least of having to find good homes for them. However, if she does get loose and is mated, take her immediately to your vet who will be able to give an injection to prevent her producing puppies.

A bitch comes into season at six-monthly intervals, each time for 18–21 days. However, she is only fertile for three to five days of this period. The rest of the time she will attract neighbourhood dogs if they scent her. Therefore, when you take her for walks and if she is small enough, carry her 20 or so paces from your front gate before putting her down. When returning, carry her a similar distance to your gate. During this period, bitches may become sexually excited and pursue dogs aggressively.

Dabbing the bitch's paws with a strongly scented substance, such as oil of lavender, will help to put dogs off her scent.

• **Neutering**: If you have no intention of breeding your pet, it is possible to make a dog's or bitch's life happier and more contented by removing their sexual drive. In a dog it will make him less prone to wandering and chasing neighbourhood bitches, and with a bitch it will free her – and you – of the problems that arise when she is in season.

Neutering is a simple operation carried out under a general anaesthetic. Bitches are 'spayed', which involves the removal of the womb and ovaries. In a male dog the testicles are removed, a process known as castration.

A veterinary surgeon should be consulted and advice taken about the best age to undertake this neutering. In general, castration is usually undertaken when a dog is sexually mature and this can be any time between the ages of six months and 18 months, depending on the breed. A bitch is usually allowed to be in season once before being spayed, although this proviso has been in debate recently.

If either a dog or bitch is neutered too early, there is a chance of the animal becoming fat, but if undertaken at the right time there should not be a change in character.

> ### House-proud factor
>
> If you are house-proud, it is likely that a puppy or dog is not for you. A puppy turns a house into a home, but be prepared for doggy smells, hairs on furniture, stains on carpets and the problem of drying wet towels after wiping a dog's coat immediately after coming home and out of the rain. Although the smell of a wet dog is ambrosic to many people, it can be nauseating to others.
>
> A 'trophy dog' to impress neighbours should never be a consideration (see page 22).

## When is the right time to have a puppy?

Most puppies and dogs are highly adaptable, but where possible do not arrange to introduce a new puppy into your life and household when major changes are happening. Moving to a new home, the arrival of a baby, Christmas celebrations or a change of partner soon disorientates a puppy, causing stress and uncertainty.

Where possible, only introduce a puppy into your home when there is an everyday routine that the new arrival can get to know quickly and accept as a normal way of life. Also, the time of year has an influence on training and settling in a puppy, and the best time is in spring or early summer.

*All puppies and dogs like to have a toy to gnaw.*

## Social needs of puppies – and dogs

Puppies and dogs delight in being part of a family's social activities – and especially if the centre of attention!

● **Puppies and dogs need company**: Dogs are pack animals and become unhappy if left too much on their own or for long periods. They are sensitive creatures and if neglected soon become stressed. If you cannot offer a puppy or dog time for play and exercise, it is better to consider another pet.

● **Space available**: When selecting a puppy, check that when it grows up you have sufficient space to make life a pleasure. A dog needs a day-area as well as one at night. Often, when a family goes to bed, the dog settles into a basket; he then assumes a protective role. All of this demands space.

● **Is your garden escape-proof?**: Puppies are like eels in the way they try to squeeze through and under a boundary fence.

Puppy-proofing fences, hedges and gates is detailed in the chapter on 'Household and garden dangers', page 166.

● **Regular exercise**: Ensure you have time to take your dog for a walk at least once a day and, preferably, twice. The amount of exercise needed depends on the breed. Labrador Retrievers, German Shepherd Dogs and Collies need plenty of exercise to keep them healthy and ensure their minds stay active. Smaller breeds – especially miniature types – will probably get sufficient exercise by wandering around a garden, but this rather insular exercise does not increase their socializing skills with other dogs and people. With age, a dog requires less exercise at each walk than when young. The general health of a dog also influences its need for exercise, especially if it has developed mobility problems due to old age. Do not force a dog to undertake long walks when it is clear it is becoming difficult for him. Before a dog can be taken for regular walks, he needs to have been trained when a puppy to walk on a lead and to react to commands (see pages 100–107).

*When young, puppies may appear to be 'all legs', but they soon grow into properly proportioned animals.*

### Trophy dogs

Sadly, a few prospective owners of dogs see them as status symbols and perhaps as a way to bolster inadequacies in their own character and lifestyle. These include 'handbag' dogs, originally bought as a fashion accessory, later to be 'dumped' when styles change. Many large breeds are also initially kept as walk-about trophies, but when the cost of feeding becomes apparent they are abandoned.

Other status dogs are those kept by owners who seek to make a 'macho' statement. Eventually, many of these dogs are abandoned or passed to animal rescue societies for rehoming. Unfortunately, dogs which have lived as sidekicks to macho exhibitionists are difficult to rehome and often have to be put to sleep.

*A Beagle puppy playing in winter sunshine on a deserted beach.*

# Where to buy a puppy

There are several avenues to finding a puppy – or young dog – that suits you and your family. You may have your mind set on a pedigree breed, and therefore the wide range of different breeds detailed on pages 32–85 will help to clarify your thoughts. Or you may be flexible in your ideas and feel a cross-breed or mongrel would be better. Indeed, mongrel puppies and dogs are often healthier than pure-bred types which, through selective breeding, may have debilitating characteristics. From whichever source you obtain a puppy or dog, ensure you gain information on the animal's diet and the type and brand of food currently being eaten. This will help a puppy or dog settle into your home more easily.

*When puppies are old enough to leave their mother it can be a stressful time for them.*

*Make sure any animal you intend to buy has been medically checked by a vet; it should be able to eat and drink.*

Detailed here are the main sources of puppies and dogs.

## Buying from an animal rescue society

Increasingly, animal welfare societies have unwanted puppies and dogs that need new and caring homes.

● The range of backgrounds of these animals is wide: they may have been mistreated, proved too expensive to keep or rejected on a whim and cast aside in favour of another dog.

● Animal welfare rescue societies take these animals into their care, check their health and welfare and assess them for rehoming.

● These are puppies and dogs that when adopted by a family more than repay the kindness, food and security offered to them. The authors of this book have first-hand experience of having a young, rescued Labrador-Collie cross and cannot talk too highly about its success – she was adored by the entire family, including six cats.

● Rescue societies make a charge when rehoming an animal to cover some of the cost incurred while caring for it. Before offering a puppy or dog to a family, rescue societies establish their suitability to have an animal. Also, later, they often carry out further home visits to ensure the animal has settled into its new home.

● Most rescue organizations will insist that the animal is neutered, if this is not already the case.

● These are animals that need special care when being rehomed. Their confidence of being with people in a home will have been eroded and initially they may not have the temperament to adjust quickly to a new environment.

● Welcoming a puppy or dog into your home is described on pages 88–95, but great sensitivity is needed when dealing with a rescued animal. If he annoys you or is disobedient, do not shout at him. It is probable that he does not understand what you want – and that is your fault! It is love and patience, combined with a routine, that he understands and this will, eventually, be successful.

*A puppy peering through wire-netting is appealing – but only buy one that is healthy and old enough to leave its mother.*

*Close rapport between a mother and her puppy is instantly apparent in this picture.*

Choosing a puppy or dog

## Buying from a dog breeder

It is best to buy from a dog breeder who specializes in the particular breed you want, rather than from a general breeding kennel. Local vets will be able to suggest an appropriate kennel. If not, contact the club specializing in the breed you want and ask for details of reputable local breeders.

● After making contact with a possible breeding kennel, make a visit to ensure the establishment is reputable. Check that it is clean, with no stale food or signs of excrement or urine.

● If the owners are reluctant to show you over the premises, try another place. The entire breeding establishment must reveal signs of 'caring' and 'cleanliness', with staff looking happy and full of vitality.

● Ask to see the mother of the litter; if she wags her tail, this is a good sign that the puppy will also be friendly. Don't choose a puppy from a mother who is snappy and surly.

● If the kennel's owner asks about you and your ability to look after a puppy, this is a good sign that the establishment cares for their puppies and it is not just a financial transaction.

● Confirm with the kennel's owner that the puppy has been given the correct injections for its age.

● Ensure you are given any pedigree papers that apply.

### Buying from a pet shop

This method often appears convenient and appealing, especially if a puppy nudges up to a street window and wags its tail at you. However, resist the temptation to buy. The majority of these animals come from puppy farms and many have problems. Added to this, you will not know of the mother's disposition.

*Always choose the brightest and happiest puppy.*

## Buying from a friend

This can be an excellent way to obtain a puppy and one often undertaken through friends-of-friends or children's schoolfriends, as well as close and long-term friends.

● You should be allowed to visit the puppy's mother and see her size as well as making an assessment of her friendliness and interaction with children.

● If a mongrel, you may not be sure of the animal's eventual size, but as an indication of what to expect have a look at his paws; if large, the dog will also be big.

● Puppies bought from a friend – or through friends – are usually able to make the change from one home to another very easily, whereas puppies raised in kennels are being moved into an environment that is alien to them.

● You will be able to find out from the owners the date when you can take the puppy home – ensure you are prepared with feeding and water bowls, as well as a basket, ready for the exciting new arrival.

● Don't be tempted in any circumstances to select the runt of the litter – it is never successful.

# Matching personalities

It has long been acknowledged that some breeds of dog bear amusing resemblances to their owners – perhaps their walk, dress or general decorum. It is also said that if owners and their dogs are seen separately it is possible to match them up, based solely on their appearances!

However, recent research at an English university now suggests that the choice of breed also reflects the owner's personality. For example:

● **Gundogs**: Includes Setters, Pointers, Retrievers and Spaniels. Indicates – highly agreeable.

● **Hounds**: Hunting dogs range from long-legged breeds which hunt by using their sight, including Afghan, Borzoi and Greyhounds, to those with shorter legs which hunt by following a scent, such as Beagles (a gregarious and popular hunting pack breed) and Bloodhounds. Indicates – high emotional stability.

*Spaniels are friendly, agreeable and lively dogs that spread fun and happiness. They delight in being the centre of attraction.*

*Italian Greyhounds resemble miniature greyhounds; they are highly active and often kept by intelligent, creative people.*

*Bearded Collies have a rustic and relaxed nature. They are independent and indicate an highly extrovert owner.*

*Pomeranians are a miniature breed, with a dainty nature and distinctive appearance that appeals to creative owners.*

- **Miniature and toy breeds**: Include King Charles Spaniels and Pekingese. Indicates – high intelligence and creativity.

- **Pastoral breeds**: Includes Collies, The Old English Sheepdog and the Welsh Corgi. Indicates – highly extrovert.

- **Utility breeds (service dogs)**: These are non-sporting breeds and do not fall into hunting and working groups, but include well-known breeds such as Dalmatian, Bulldog and Keeshond. Indicates – highly conscientious.

*These Bulldog puppies will develop into stocky, pugnacious adults and be ideal for owners who are very conscientious.*

Judging personality traits can be either depressing or elating, but, whatever the judgement of this survey, remember that research indicates that most owners of dogs are happy, friendly and affable people.

# Lost or found

Occasionally your treasured puppy or dog will escape from your garden, or you may find an escapee wandering along a road or across a recreational field. These are realistic facts of having a puppy or dog – but what should you do if you find yourself in either of these worrying circumstances?

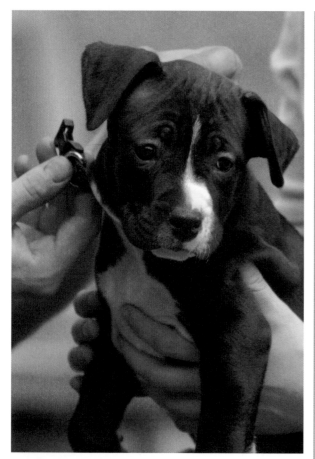

*Losing a puppy or dog can be just as distressing for the animal itself as for the owner.*

## If you find a stray animal

Legally, a stray dog is 'one that is in a public place and not under the control of a keeper'. There are several ways to ensure the animal is returned to its owner, including:

● Report the matter to a dog warden or relevant officer working for the local authority.

● If you decide to take responsibility for a stray animal you must, by law, either return the animal to its owner (assuming such a person can be identified from information on the dog's collar), or contact your local authority and explain the circumstances to them (such as date, time and place). Sometimes, a dog warden will collect the animal from you.

● Whatever you do, remember that it is illegal for you to retain the animal without written permission from the local authority or the police.

## If you lose a puppy or dog

● Ring your local council and the police and give them full details – date, place, age of dog, breed or type of dog.

● If, after contacting your local council and police, the puppy or dog appears or is returned to you, contact these authorities again to inform them so that their time is not wasted by making further investigations.

● Search sheds and garages to check the animal has not wandered into them and fallen asleep.

*Stray puppies appear to need a home, but there is a legal code for them (see below).*

• Knock on neighbouring doors to see if the animal has been noticed. Also, circulate a picture and note about the puppy or dog to other houses in your neighbourhood, and try local kennels, vets and animal sanctuaries.

## Legal code for strays

Under the Environment Protection Act 1990, your local council is legally responsible for dealing with stray dogs.

• It is no longer the responsibility of the police to accept stray animals, although they have to record reports of lost animals notified to them by the general public.

• Local authorities are obliged to provide kennelling for dogs seized by its officers or brought in by anyone else. They are obliged to keep the animal for a minimum of seven days, if not claimed by the owner.

• Local authorities can charge owners of stray dogs any cost incurred in collecting and keeping the dog. Additionally, they are obliged to keep a register of dogs they have seized, which the public can inspect free of charge.

• Under the Clean Neighbourhood and Environment Act 2005, local authorities are obliged to provide an out-of-hours telephone number for the public to use should they come across a stray dog.

• Under the law, a pet dog must wear a collar when in a public area, with the owner's name and contact details.

# RANGE OF BREEDS

# Which breed is suitable?

Everyone has their own favourite breed of dog, perhaps one known from childhood, seen in a friend's house or even casually noticed while out for a walk. Dogs can be classified in several ways and one is by their size (see pages 36–37), which gives a quick idea about the space a particular breed needs.

Another way to classify them is into types and uses of breeds, such as gundogs, terriers and pastoral breeds, as well as miniature and toy types. There are some dogs, however, that do not neatly fall into these groups and include breeds such as Boxer, Newfoundland and Dalmatian.

Whatever a breed's classification, the majority of them are featured in this detailed and abundantly illustrated pageant of breeds.

*'A house is not a home without a dog' is an often-made claim – and for many people it is quite correct.*

## Family dogs

Several breeds of dog are well known for their affectionate and friendly dispositions, especially with young children who invariably create a 'rough and tumble' home environment. Some families traditionally have the same breed of dog from one generation to another and this is reassuring as it must be trustworthy with youngsters.

In general, breeds most suitable to family life are small to medium-sized ones, such as many terriers, retrievers and spaniels. However, larger breeds, including Afghans, German Shepherd Dogs and Old English Sheepdogs, are remarkably tolerant of children. Miniature and toy breeds are usually too small and delicate to be family pets in homes where there are very small children.

If you are new to having a dog in your family's life, ask other families about the dog breed they have and whether it is a good companion for small children.

Ways to introduce puppies and dogs to households, and especially to children, are explained in the chapter on 'Introducing a puppy to your home', page 86.

# Cross-breeds and mongrels

Many people prefer to have a cross-breed or mongrel as a family pet as usually they are healthier and fitter than pedigree types. Unfortunately, some pedigree breeds now suffer from too much inbreeding during earlier years, resulting in physical problems. Fortunately, extensive work is now being carried out to try to rectify them. Therefore, do not discount cross-breeds and mongrels as not being suitable pets. They may not, in some people's minds, be 'trendy' and 'voguish', but as family pets they can be superb.

## Cross-breeds

These are animals whose dams and sires belong to two different pure breeds. Their eventual physical appearance and nature often can be guessed at – but without certainty as the genes of the parents inevitably reconfigure in different ways in each of their puppies.

Some dog breeders create cross-breeds from specific pedigree breeds. These dogs, usually referred to as 'designer' dogs, are often called by an amalgam of their parents' names, such as 'Cockerpoo' (Cocker Spaniel and Poodle), 'Puggle' (Pug and Beagle), and 'Labradoodle' (Labrador and Poodle).

These are bred because the progeny often make excellent family dogs. For example, a Labrador-Collie cross has many of the outstanding attributes of its parents and is very popular as a family pet. For a specific type of cross-breed, talk with your vet (who will know of local dog breeders producing cross-breeds) or visit an animal welfare society.

## Mongrels

These are animals with several different breeds in their parentage, and because of their diversity of genes they do not usually suffer from the inherited congenital disorders which plague many pedigree breeds. Mongrels are superb family dogs and animal welfare societies are excellent sources for them. They usually have dogs in every size and shape!

*A family dog will change your life, encouraging you to take more personal exercise.*

Don't discount having a puppy or dog just because its ears, feet or tail appear unusual or amusing; such animals are full of fun and have characters that will endear them to you throughout their lives.

# Classifying dogs by size

Some breeds, such as Great Danes and Newfoundlands, are the giants of the dog world, while miniature and toy breeds are much smaller and better suited for small houses. Detailed here is a range of breeds, with indications of their height to the shoulder and approximate weight. However, weights usually vary between dogs and bitches, as well as being influenced by the age of the animal – in middle age, weight sometimes increases, while in old age it often decreases. Therefore, the weight groupings given for the following breeds are an approximation, but nevertheless provide an indication of size.

**Giant breeds**
These are large and require generous feeding, plenty of space indoors and long walks. They are heavy, in the region of 36–84 kg (80–185 lb), expensive to feed and with life spans usually shorter than smaller breeds.
★ Bloodhound (see page 40)
★ Bullmastiff (see page 80)
★ Deerhound (see page 41)
★ Great Dane (see page 82)
★ Irish Wolfhound (see page 43)
★ Newfoundland (see page 82)
★ Pyrenean Mountain Dog (see page 66)
★ Saint Bernard (see page 84)

**Large breeds**
Smaller than giant breeds, but nevertheless large, they weigh 23–36 kg (50–80 lb). Some have become working dogs, involved in security and herding animals.
★ Afghan Hound (see page 38)
★ Borzoi (see page 40)
★ Boxer (see page 79)
★ Briard (see page 63)
★ Clumber Spaniel (see page 56)
★ Collie (see page 64)
★ Collie, Bearded (see page 64)
★ Collie, Smooth-coated (see page 64)
★ Curly-coated Retriever (see page 57)
★ Dobermann Pinscher (see page 81)
★ English Setter (see page 57)
★ Flat-coated Retriever (see page 58)
★ German Shepherd Dog (see page 65)
★ Golden Retriever (see page 59)
★ Gordon Setter (see page 59)
★ Greyhound (see page 43)
★ Irish Setter (see page 60)
★ Irish Water Spaniel (see page 60)
★ Labrador Retriever (see page 61)
★ Old English Sheepdog (see page 65)
★ Pointer (see page 62)
★ Rhodesian Ridgeback (see page 44)
★ Rottweiler (see page 66)
★ Weimaraner (see page 85)

## Medium breeds

These are popular and several make wonderful family dogs; they weigh 13.5–23 kg (30–50 lb).

★ Airedale Terrier (see page 46)
★ Australian Heeler (see page 63)
★ Basset Hound (see page 39)
★ Bulldog (see page 80)
★ Bull Terrier (see page 48)
★ Chow Chow (see page 80)
★ Dalmatian (see page 81)
★ Elkhound (see page 42)
★ English Springer Spaniel (see page 58)
★ Finnish Spitz (see page 42)
★ Keeshond (see page 82)
★ Kerry Blue Terrier (see page 50)
★ Poodle (see page 83)
★ Portuguese Water Dog (see page 83)
★ Saluki (see page 44)
★ Samoyed (see page 84)
★ Schnauzer (see page 85)
★ Staffordshire Bull Terrier (see page 54)
★ Sussex Spaniel (see page 62)

## Small breeds

Many of these are ideal as family pets where space is limited. They weigh 4.5–13.5 kg (10–30 lb).

★ Australian Terrier (see page 46)
★ Basenji (see page 38)
★ Beagle (see page 39)
★ Bedlington Terrier (see page 47)
★ Border Terrier (see page 47)
★ Boston Terrier (see page 48)
★ Cairn Terrier (see page 49)
★ Cocker Spaniel (see page 57)
★ Dachshund, Long-haired (see page 41)
★ Dachshund, Smooth-haired (see page 41)
★ Dachshund, Wire-coated (see page 41)
★ Dandie Dinmont Terrier (see page 49)
★ Irish Terrier (see page 50)
★ Lakeland Terrier (see page 51)

★ Lhasa Apso (see page 72)
★ Manchester Terrier (page 51)
★ Schipperke (see page 76)
★ Scottish Terrier (see page 52)
★ Sealyham Terrier (see page 52)
★ Shetland Sheepdog (see page 77)
★ Shih Tzu (see page 78)
★ Skye Terrier (see page 53)
★ Smooth-haired Fox Terrier (see page 53)
★ Welsh Corgi, Cardiganshire (see page 67)
★ Welsh Corgi, Pembrokeshire (see page 67)
★ Welsh Springer Spaniel (see page 67)
★ Welsh Terrier (see page 54)
★ West Highland White Terrier (see page 55)
★ Whippet (see page 45)
★ Wire-haired Fox Terrier (see page 55)

## Miniature and toy breeds

These are small dogs; many were developed to be lapdogs. They weigh 1–4.5 kg (2–10 lb).

★ Affenpinscher (see page 68)
★ Cavalier King Charles Spaniel (see page 68)
★ Chihuahua (see page 69)
★ Chinese Crested Dog (see page 70)
★ Griffon (see page 70)
★ Italian Greyhound (see page 71)
★ Japanese Spaniel (see page 71)
★ King Charles Spaniel (see page 72)
★ Maltese (see page 73)
★ Miniature Bull Terrier (see page 73)
★ Miniature Long-haired Dachshund (see page 73)
★ Miniature Pinscher (see page 73)
★ Miniature Poodle (see page 74)
★ Miniature Schnauzer (see page 74)
★ Miniature Smooth-haired Dachshund (see page 74)
★ Papillon (see page 74)
★ Pekingese (see page 75)
★ Pomeranian (see page 75)
★ Pug (see page 76)
★ Yorkshire Terrier (see page 78)

# Hounds

These popular breeds can be divided into two groups. First there are the ones with long legs which run fast and detect prey by sight. Second are those with shorter legs which are slower and hunt by following a scent. Hounds have a wide range of heritages, originating in many regions of the world including Russia, Africa, North America and Europe. Each breed has a distinctive character and attitude to life.

## Afghan Hound

Dignified and aloof breed, whose ancestors can be traced to 5,000 or more years ago when they were familiar among Egyptian royalty. Originally, this distinctive breed was developed and trained for hunting in hilly regions.

Besides being excellent hunters, this breed makes a good family pet, with the merits of seldom barking and possessing a gentle nature. Afghan Hounds are so distinctive that everywhere they go they are noticed – their heads and tails held high and walking with a springy gait.

Colours vary but they are usually red, fawn, golden or black-and-tan. The coat is silky, naturally short on the back but long on the flanks, ears and limbs. They are about 72 cm (28 in) high at the shoulder and weigh 29.5 kg (65 lb).

*The Basenji is alert and can trot like a horse.*

## Basenji

Earlier known as the Congo Bush Dog and Belgian Congo Dog, it is rare in the dog world in that it does not bark – only occasionally offering something akin to a squeal or soft growl.

The breed was widely used in southern Sudan and old Belgian Congo (now the Democratic Republic of the Congo) to hunt wounded game. It has a keen and sensitive nose for detecting game, and is active and fast-running.

Ancestors of this breed can be traced back about 3,000 or more years, when they were depicted in rock drawings.

The usual colour is chestnut, with white points (colours on face, ears, legs and tail), and a smooth, short coat. They are usually 40 cm (16 in) high and weigh about 9 kg (20 lb).

*The Afghan Hound has an elegant bearing.*

*The Basset Hound displays a determined expression.*

## Basset Hound

Most people know what a Basset Hound looks like from the famous 'Fred Basset' cartoon series featuring this distinctive breed, where he is made to look quite human, with a superior attitude and 'don't bother me' expression. However, these dogs have also come to be popular through their good-natured disposition with children, as they are slow to anger.

The breed is descended from an old western European race of badger-hunting dogs and was introduced into the British Isles in the 1860s.

They are usually tri-coloured (black, white and tan) or white and roan, with a short, fine and close coat. Of course, their trademark is their long, supple, velvety ears. They usually weigh 20 kg (45 lb) and are about 32 cm (13 in) at the shoulder.

## Beagle

A gregarious and alert breed said to be native to the British Isles and earlier used for hunting rabbits. Now they are generally employed for hunting in packs, where their stamina and active nature are utilized.

The Beagle is usually seen in 'hound' colours, a mixture of black, tan and white. The coat is short but dense, sometimes wiry. They usually weigh about 13–15 kg (30–35 lb) and stand 35 cm (14 in) high at the shoulder.

*The Beagle is one of the most sociable breeds.*

## Bloodhound

This breed deserves to be more popular as they are exceptionally affectionate and friendly, with no sign of a quarrelsome nature. Additionally, they are agreeable among other breeds. They are powerful but usually shy, with loose skin hanging in deep folds about the neck.

Their coat colour is variable, black-and-tan, red-and-tan, or tawny. Sometimes the glossy coat is flecked in white, with a small amount of white on the chest and feet.

Bloodhounds are part of an ancient breed, said to have been introduced into the British Isles by the Normans, nearly a thousand years ago. However, at that time they were a big, black hound; the modern Bloodhound is thought to be a descendant of the St Hubert Hound, the Talbot and an old southern hound.

Their powers of detecting and following a scent are legendary, tracking felons and even apprehending miscreants individually amid large crowds. Because this breed was either owned by titled people or used by law enforcers for tracking, it became known as Bloodhound.

Puppies are slow to mature; they result in animals weighing about 45 kg (100 lb) and 66 cm (26 in) high at the shoulder.

*The Borzoi can show an impressive turn of speed.*

## Borzoi

This elegant, wolf-hunting breed, sometimes known as the Russian Wolfhound, Russian Greyhound or Siberian Wolfhound, was imported into the British Isles in the mid-1870s. It was kept for hunting and other sporting activities by the Russian tsars and is famed for its bravery, muscular power and speed.

It is a beautiful breed, with a graceful and aristocratic appearance and long, silky coat that is flat, wavy or slightly curled. Its tail is set low, abundantly 'clothed', and when the animal is running and turning or moving rapidly it acts as a rudder to maintain stability at speed.

At first glance, the Borzoi's head appears too small for its body, but this is deceptive and, together with the animal's Roman nose, it creates a distinctive and beautiful feature.

The long, silky coat is usually white with red, orange or lemon markings. It is not less than 73 cm (29 in) at the shoulder and weighs about 36 kg (80 lb).

*The Bloodhound has an 'old gentleman' facial appearance.*

*Dachshunds have an inquisitive and playful nature.*

# Dachshund

The term Dachshund in German means 'badger dog' and it was during the 17th century that a dog similar to the one we know today came to the attention of hunters. The dog's speciality was pursuing badgers down holes, but it was also used against foxes and wounded deer. They make wonderful pets, being highly intelligent and very playful.

There are three types of Dachshund: the Long-haired Dachshund, the Smooth-haired Dachshund, and the Wire-coated Dachshund.

• **The Long-haired Dachshund** has a soft and straight, or slightly waved, coat, which tends to be longer around the neck and on the underparts. The colour of the shiny coat is variable and can be black-and-tan, dark brown with lighter shadings, dark red, light red, dappled, tiger-marked or brindle.

It is a distinctive, long, low-to-the-ground breed, being 23–25 cm (9–10 in) at the shoulder and weighing 8–11 kg (18–25 lb). However, Long-haired Dachshunds are sometimes further classified by weight: middleweight up to 7.7 kg (17 lb) for bitches, and 8 kg (18 lb) for dogs; heavyweight over 7.7 kg (17 lb) for bitches and over 8 kg (18 lb) for dogs.

• **The Smooth-haired Dachshund** has a short, dense coat, in any colour other than white, although a white spot can often be seen on the breast. Dogs should not exceed 11 kg (25 lb) in weight, bitches 10 kg (23 lb).

• **The Wire-coated Dachshund** is the least common of the Dachshund group and, with the exception of its jaw, eyebrows and ears, the body is completely covered with a short, even, wiry coat. There is a range of colours – usually iron or steel grey – and it has a characteristic beard and bushy eyebrows. Dogs weigh 9–10 kg (20–22 lb), bitches 8–9 kg (18–20 lb).

They are superb trackers; good sight and scent detection.

*The Deerhound is an aristocrat among dogs.*

# Deerhound

Doubtless, this is one of the ancient dogs of the British Isles and was formerly used for hunting deer in the Scottish Highlands. This earned the breed the titles Scottish Deerhound, Scottish Wolfhound, Staghound, Scotch Greyhound and Royal Dog of Scotland; it goes back to the 16th century when it was a favourite among Scottish chieftains. Such was the value put on the breed that a brace of them could ransom a nobleman.

A deerhound's coat is harsh, wiry and 7.5–10 cm (3–4 in) long. However, hair on the face and belly is softer. Overall, the coat is thick, somewhat ragged and close-lying, and harsh or crisp to the touch. Coat colours include grey, dark blue-grey, brindle and wheaten.

It is a large breed, with dogs no less than 76 cm (30 in) at the shoulder and bitches 72 cm (28 in). In weight, dogs are 38–47 kg (85–105 lb) and bitches 29–36 kg (65–80 lb).

*The Elkhound has an alert and active nature.*

## Elkhound

A strong and powerful breed, earlier well known in Norway and Sweden. Its ancestors were used to herd flocks and defend villagers from wolves, as well as for hunting elk. It belongs to the Spitz group of breeds.

These dogs have a will of their own and anyone thinking of owning one should be experienced in training dogs. However, it is a friendly and intelligent breed, with great energy and independence of character and without any sign of nervousness.

Elkhounds require plenty of exercise each day in a place where they can run free.

The breed has a compact and, proportionately, short body, with a thick coat, pricked-up ears and a tail tightly curled over its back. The coat's normal colour is grey, with black tips to the long outer areas. Usually, the colour on the chest, stomach, legs and underside of the tail is lighter.

It is a heavy breed and dogs often weigh 23 kg (50 lb) and bitches 19 kg (43 lb). Height also varies – dogs are 52 cm (20 in) at the shoulder and bitches are slightly less, standing 45 cm (18 in) high.

## Finnish Spitz

Finland has provided the dog world with a handsome breed and one with the characteristics of eagerness to hunt, courage and fidelity. It belongs to the Spitz group of breeds and is one of the earliest to have been domesticated. This is a superb family dog and moderately easy to train.

It is a muscular breed, with a thick and dense coat. The back is reddish-brown or yellowish-red, with hairs on the inner sides of the ears, cheeks, underneath the muzzle, on the breast, abdomen and inside the legs a lighter shade.

At shoulder height, males are 44–50 cm (17–20 in), while bitches are 39–45 cm (15–18 in). They weigh about 15 kg (35 lb).

*The Finnish Spitz has an independent attitude.*

*Greyhounds are ideal as family pets.*

## Greyhound

Few people cannot recognize a greyhound, a breed famed for being the fastest in the world and trained to pursue a mechanical hare around a track for the financial gain or loss for thousands of people each year. Apart from its remarkable stamina and endurance – with a near legendary long-reaching leg movement – it is a superb family pet, easily adapting to home life during retirement from sport.

Each year, many are bred for the racing industry and specially trained to perform on the track, but only a few are successful. The ones not required are either killed or passed on for rehoming. Even those animals which are successful on the track have a relatively short career before they, too, become unwanted and are either despatched or rehomed through charities such as the Retired Greyhound Trust.

These are reserved, cautious and highly strung animals and when kept as pets appear only to want to lounge on a settee or be close to a roaring fire in winter.

It is an ancient breed, probably of Egyptian origin and bred in Britain for at least a thousand years. It is seen in many colour variations, including black, white, red, blue, fawn, fallow or brindle, or any of these colours broken with white. The coat is short and smooth.

The ideal height for dogs is 72–75 cm (28–30 in) at the shoulder, and bitches 68–72 cm (27–28 in). They usually weigh about 30 kg (65 lb).

## Irish Wolfhound

A noble, muscular and especially large Irish hunting breed, that is claimed to have been kept at the ancient courts of Irish kings. Although large, it should not be as heavy and massive as the Great Dane.

For all its size, it is an elegant and graceful breed, with a head and neck carried high and with an upward, aristocratic sweep. It is not aggressive and makes a wonderful family dog if you have sufficient room indoors and are able to provide it with plenty of exercise.

The colour of its rough-textured coat – especially wiry and long over its eyes and under the jaw – is variable from animal to animal. You may see it in grey, brindle, red, black, pure white or fawn. Usually, however, it is brindle or fawn.

The average height at the shoulder for dogs is 78 cm (31 in), and bitches 72 cm (28 in). Dogs weigh about 54 kg (120 lb) and bitches 40 kg (90 lb).

*The Irish Wolfhound is noble and courageous.*

*The Rhodesian Ridgeback has a distinctive coat.*

## Rhodesian Ridgeback

A distinctive breed, also known as the African Lion Hound or Rhodesian Lion-dog. The ridge on its back is formed by hair growing in the opposite direction to the rest of the coat. This ridge, about 5 cm (2 in) wide, is clearly defined, starting behind the shoulders and continuing to the hip bones.

A few people claim that the presence of this ridge makes a dog more likely to suffer from dermoid sinus. This is a debilitating genetic disorder which can result in meningitis and myelitis, causing spinal pain, rigidity and fever; it can be life-threatening.

One in 20 puppies is born with no ridge and at one time the code of ethics of the Rhodesian Ridgeback Club stated that they should be culled. However, this has since been amended and ridgeless pups are now sold as pets rather than being used as potential show dogs.

The origin of the breed goes back many hundreds of years to when German, Dutch and French Huguenots emigrated to South Africa. The dogs they took with them mated with half-wild native dogs, producing the ancestors of the breed we know today.

It is a muscular, strong and active breed, making an excellent guard dog; it is capable of great endurance and has a good turn of speed. It is a breed best handled by one person.

The coat is short, dense, sleek and glossy, but neither silky nor woolly. In colour it is light-wheaten to red-wheaten.

It is a relatively heavy breed and dogs are 36 kg (80 lb), bitches 31 kg (70 lb). Dogs are 63–68 cm (25–27 in) high at the shoulder, bitches 60–66 cm (24–26 in).

## Saluki

Known as the Gazelle Hound, it is claimed to be an old Arabian breed used for hunting gazelles. It is also thought to be the Royal Dog of Egypt and said to have been a distinct breed more than 2,300 years ago.

It is an athletic-looking breed with an active nature, great speed and endurance; at the same time, it appears graceful and dignified.

*The Saluki has an athletic and graceful nature.*

The Saluki's coat is smooth, short and silky, with slight feathering on the legs and backs of the thighs. There are several distinct colours, including white, cream, fawn, golden, red, grizzle-and-tan, black-and-tan, and tri-coloured (white, black and tan).

Dogs are 58–72 cm (23–28 in) at the shoulder, with bitches slightly less. The average weight is 25 kg (55 lb).

## Whippet

A northern English breed developed for coursing during the 1850s. Sometimes known as the Working Man's Greyhound, it is the fastest dog in the world for its weight, with speeds up to 56 km per hour (35 miles per hour).

It was used by miners for rabbiting and later trained to run a 183 m (200 yd) course, with dogs frequently covering this distance in 12 seconds.

The Whippet has a beautifully balanced nature, with plenty of muscular power and strength combined with charming grace and elegance.

The coat is short and especially smooth, in any colour or a mixture of colours.

The ideal height for dogs is 45 cm (18 in) at the shoulder, and 43 cm (17 in) for bitches. They usually weigh about 9.5 kg (21 lb).

*Whippets are known for their fast acceleration.*

# Terriers

These are breeds that owe their name to the Latin word for 'earth' – *terra*. Initially, they were used on farms to search out underground vermin, but are now usually kept as pets for their bright and lively disposition.

## Airedale Terrier

This is the largest of all the terriers and it has a bright and friendly disposition. They appear to walk on tiptoe, with expectancy of imminent movement. Additionally, they are good with children.

They were bred in Yorkshire, England, in the 1870s and take their name from the River Aire. It is said that the breed was originated to keep down the large number of rats around Bradford, Bingley and Otley, and locally the breed became known as Waterside Terriers and Working Terriers.

Their coat should be hard, dense and wiry, close to the body and legs, and without a ragged texture. The head and ears, with the exception of dark markings on each side of the skull, should be tan. The ears are a slightly darker colour.

This is a large breed, with dogs 58–60 cm (23–24 in) in height at the shoulder and bitches 55–58 cm (22–23 in). They weigh about 23 kg (50 lb).

*The Australian Terrier has an alert and determined nature.*

## Australian Terrier

This is the smallest breed of the terrier group, with an ancestry that goes back to 1885 when it was first shown in a dog show in Melbourne, Australia. They have a low, compact and active nature.

Australian Terriers are keen and alert, easy to handle and ideal as town dogs as well as in the country.

There are two colour forms: the first is a blue or silver-grey body, tan-coloured on legs and face, with a blue or silver top-knot; the second is sandy or red, with a softer-coloured top-knot. The coat is straight, hard-textured and 5–6 cm (2–2¹/₂ in) long.

The average weight is 4.5–5 kg (10–11 lb), and they are about 25 cm (10 in) in height at the shoulder.

*The Airedale Terrier is known as the 'king of terriers'.*

## Bedlington Terrier

A distinctive terrier that inhabited the borders of England and Scotland during the early part of the 1800s, where they were used for otter and badger hunting. Claims are made that the breed evolved from gypsy dogs in Northumberland, a county in the north of England.

Animals are muscular, lithe and graceful, with a pear- or wedge-shaped head and an expression of repose. Usually, they are mild and gentle, though neither nervous nor shy, but when roused full of courage and with a sparkle in their eyes. They have a springy gait and are capable of running at great speed.

The thick coat, which stands out from the skin, is blue, blue-and-tan, liver, or sandy. Animals are about 40 cm (16 in) at the shoulder, and weigh 8–10 kg (18–23 lb).

*The Bedlington Terrier was originally a poacher's dog.*

## Border Terrier

This is a working terrier, able to follow horses and combine activity with gameness. They take their name from the area around the English and Scottish borders and are thought to be associated with the Dandie Dinmont and Bedlington breeds. The breed is at least 350 years old.

They have a deep and narrow but fairly long body, with a harsh and dense coat. There are several colour variations, including red, wheaten, grizzle-and-tan, and blue-and-tan.

Dogs usually weigh 5.8–7 kg (13–15 lb), bitches 5.2–6.3 kg (11–14 lb). The average height at the shoulder is 31 cm (12 in).

*The Border Terrier has a tenacious and sprightly character.*

## Boston Terrier

Known in some countries as The Boston, it is of American origin and was created from English and French Bulldogs, with terrier additions in about 1875.

It is a lively, highly intelligent, short-headed, compact and stocky breed. The coat is short and smooth, with a fine texture. Most of the body is brindle, with white markings on the muzzle and central part of the chest. Part or whole of the front legs are often covered in white, together with the back legs below the hocks.

They are usually about 38 cm (15 in) at the shoulder, and weigh around 8 kg (18 lb). Height and weight are slightly variable, from one animal to another.

## Bull Terrier

This breed looks quite ferocious but is really a most companionable dog, a family pet and reliable with children. It gained his reputation for ferocity when forced to fight in illegal pit contests. In one rat-killing contest it is claimed a Bull Terrier killed a thousand rats in a hundred minutes.

It is an old breed, known during the early to mid-1800s as the Half-and-Half and described by Pierce Egan, the famed British journalist and sportswriter. The breed was also known as the Bull-dog Terrier and the White Cavalier.

The head is oval, almost egg-shaped, long and packed with strength. Its coat is short and flat, rather harsh to the touch but with a fine gloss. The usual colour is white, but brindle forms are known.

It is 50 cm (20 in) at the shoulder and weighs 20 kg (45 lb).

*The brindle form is a Bull Terrier is popular.*

*The Boston Terrier has a lively and bright disposition.*

## Dandie Dinmont Terrier

Earlier known as the Mustard-and-Pepper Dog in the Teviotdale region of the Scottish Borders. Additionally, the breed has pet names such as Hindlee Terrier and Dandie. It was widely used for hunting otters, unearthing foxes and hunting other vermin infesting the Highlands.

This Scottish breed takes its name from the farmer Dandie Dinmont in Sir Walter Scott's story *Guy Mannering*, published in 1815. This gained the breed wider publicity; previously, it was mainly known in the Border Country.

Its pepper- or mustard-coloured coat is about 5 cm (2 in) long, not wiry but with a short and crisp feel. The pepper-coloured form ranges from a dark bluish-black to light silvery-grey, while the mustard type encompasses a reddish-brown to pale fawn.

It is relatively diminutive in size, being 20–27 cm (8–11 in) high at the shoulder and 8–11 kg (18–24 lb) in weight.

*The Cairn Terrier is an ideal family dog.*

## Cairn Terrier

This is one of the oldest Scottish terriers, originating in the Highlands of Scotland and Isle of Skye. They are smart and lively, with a terrier's fearless nature. Earlier, these dogs were used for hunting and burrowing among the cairns (rock dens in which foxes and badgers lived). Cairn Terriers have also been used indoors instead of a cat to catch mice.

Incidentally, the breed is said to be 'left-handed', a trait which has been shown in dogs to be associated with good scent detection.

They are ideal in both town and country, a loyal companion and an ideal family pet.

Their coat is profuse, hard but not coarse, and seen in several colours including wheaten, fawn, red, or light brindle; sometimes nearly black. They weigh about 6.3 kg (14 lb) and are usually 25 cm (10 in) at the shoulder.

*The Dandie Dinmont Terrier is an independent breed.*

## Irish Terrier

Sometimes known as the Irish Red Terrier, the breed is thought to have derived from black-and-tan terrier-type dogs of Britain and Ireland. Earlier, they were one of the most popular and widely known terriers and given the nickname 'Daredevil' because of their readiness to enter into a fight with other dogs. Yet their loyalty is unimpeachable and normally they are good-tempered, intelligent, excellent as a home guard, a playful friend for children and brave as a lion.

Their coat is coarse, hard and wiry, with a broken nature and free from softness or silkiness. The colour is golden-red, red-wheaten, or wheaten. Usually, there is a small patch of white on the chest.

Dogs usually weigh 12 kg (27 lb), and bitches 11 kg (25 lb), with a height at the shoulder of 45 cm (18 in).

*The wheaten-coloured form of the Irish Terrier.*

## Kerry Blue Terrier

An Irish breed, sometimes known as the Irish Blue Terrier or Kerry, thought to have been developed in County Kerry but now considered to be from Tipperary, in south-central Ireland. Originally it was used to control vermin, including rats, rabbits, badgers, foxes, otters and hares, and also to herd cattle and sheep.

The coat is a beautiful shade of blue, with puppies sometimes having a shade of tan up to the age of 18 months. Fully developed dogs weigh 15–17 kg (33–37 lb), with bitches weighing slightly less. They are usually about 45 cm (18 in) high at the shoulder.

*The Kerry Blue Terrier may reveal a surly temperament.*

*The Lakeland Terrier has an affectionate nature.*

## Lakeland Terrier

This is the smallest of the so-called long-legged terriers and it is descended from hunt terriers of the northwest English hills. Lakeland Terriers are incredibly strong for their size and completely fearless.

They have a good nature, and are energetic and playful, with a likeable disposition. Although they become devoted to one person, they make excellent family pets. It is not a yappy breed and usually only barks when there is a good reason to do so.

Their coat is dense, wiry and weather-resistant, in a range of colours: usually blue-and-tan, black-and-tan, or wheaten.

The average weight for dogs is 7.7 kg (17 lb), and for bitches slightly less at 6.8 kg (15 lb). At shoulder height the breed is about 35 cm (14 in).

## Manchester Terrier

Formerly known as the Black-and-Tan Terrier and used for rat killing and rabbit coursing in the Manchester area of England, from which it derives its name. An early form of this breed was mentioned in the 16th century, but it was then a shorter-legged dog with a rougher coat.

It has a compact appearance, with resemblance to a Whippet, which is said to be in its ancestry, together with cross-bred terriers.

The breed has an alert, upright nature, with a questioning face and fast reactions. The coat is close, short and glossy, and a combination of jet black and rich mahogany. They are sensitive to sound and inclined to bark when agitated.

Dogs weigh about 8 kg (18 lb) and bitches 7.7 kg (17 lb), with a shoulder height of 40 cm (16 in).

*The Manchester Terrier has an alert appearance.*

*The Scottish Terrier has a determined expression.*

## Scottish Terrier

This delightful and courageous terrier was known as the Aberdeen Terrier until Scotland came to regard the breed as a national treasure. Their courage earned them the title 'Die-hard'. They are dogs with a will of their own and they often try to take over a family, imposing their own desires. Nevertheless, they are superb house dogs but are best with only one master. For this reason, they are not always the best breed to have in a home with small children.

They have a sturdy, thick-set appearance and an alert nature, with short, active legs, pricked-up ears and keen eyes.

Like many other breeds, they have two coats – the undercoat is short and soft, the outer one dense and wiry. They can be seen in several different colours, including black, wheaten, grey, and brindle.

In weight they are 8.6–10 kg (19–23 lb), and to the shoulder 25–27 cm (10–11 in) high.

## Sealyham Terrier

This attractive terrier was developed in Wales and derives its name from Sealyham, in Pembrokeshire. It is not a highly active breed, displaying an even temper and relaxed character, especially as it ages.

Initially, they were bred for badger digging and have a strong, spirited nature. They make lovable and loyal family companions, but unless trained early tend to impose their own wills.

They usually have a mainly white, long and hard, wiry coat. However, sometimes the colours are white with lemon, brown, or badger markings.

In size they are about 30 cm (12 in) at the shoulder, with dogs weighing 9 kg (20 lb) and bitches 8 kg (18 lb).

*The Sealyham Terrier is tenacious and loyal.*

## Smooth-haired Fox Terrier

A popular terrier with a bright, intelligent and lively nature, which was earlier used to bolt foxes that had gone to ground. They stand alert, with an eager and slightly forward-leaning stance, full of expectancy for a command into action. Additionally, they make excellent family pets.

The coat is flat, straight and smooth, hard and dense and predominantly white.

In stature they are dominant but with medium bodyweight, a dog being 7.25–8 kg (16–18 lb) and a bitch 6.8–7.7 kg (15–17 lb). At the shoulder, the height is about 38 cm (15 in).

*A Skye Terrier was owned by Queen Victoria.*

## Skye Terrier

This breed is known to have existed in Skye and the Scottish Highlands for more than 300 years. There are also reports of dogs escaping from a Spanish shipwreck on the Isle of Skye during the 17th century and mating with local terriers, thereby creating the ancestors of the current Skye Terrier. They are independent, loyal, and best as a one-man dog, when they make a devoted friend.

It is a hardy terrier, with a low, flat coat about 13–15 cm (5–6 in) long and free from curls. They are usually dark or light blue-grey, although other colours are known, including fawn; the nose and ears should always be black.

In weight, dogs are about 11 kg (25 lb), with bitches slightly less. They are usually 25 cm (10 in) high at the shoulder, and 104 cm (41 in) long.

*The Smooth-haired Fox Terrier has a determined disposition.*

## Staffordshire Bull Terrier

During the early 1800s the English Bull Terrier was crossed with the Old English Terrier to develop a dog for use in bull pits. Later, in order to perfect the breed, breeders made a further crossing with White English Terriers and Black-and-Tan Terriers.

They are handsome dogs, with indomitable courage, high intelligence and tenacity. Their muscular body gives them great strength. Yet, for all this earlier fighting quality, they are a good family pet, being friendly and affectionate to children.

Unfortunately, they were predominantly chosen as a 'status' dog and trained to be aggressive, which has damaged their reputation and made it very difficult for animal welfare charities to rehome them.

Their coat is smooth, short and close to the skin, and comes in individual colours such as red, fawn, white, black or blue, or any of these colours with white.

They are powerful; dogs weigh 12.7–17.2 kg (28–38 lb) and bitches 10.8–15.4 kg (24–34 lb). Height at the shoulder is 35–40 cm (14–16 in).

*The Welsh Terrier is courageous and intelligent.*

## Welsh Terrier

A plucky Welsh dog, originally bred for hunting foxes, rodents and badgers but now mainly kept as a family pet; it is especially good with children. It is game and fearless, with a robust constitution.

Welsh Terriers are claimed to be one of the oldest existing breeds in the British Isles and they owe much of their parentage to the rough-haired Black-and-Tan Terriers.

Their coat is wiry, hard, close to the body and abundant. Black-and-tan is the normal colour, although black or grizzle-and-tan types are known.

Their height at the shoulder is usually 38 cm (15 in), and in weight they are 9–9.5 kg (20–21 lb).

*The Staffordshire Bull Terrier, often known as a 'Staffie'.*

## West Highland White Terrier

A plucky dog, earlier used to kill vermin and owing much of its ancestry to rough-haired Black-and-Tan Terriers. Such is the way that this popular terrier has been closely associated with Scotland that it is said to be as 'Scotch as a bagpipe'.

A small, hardy-looking terrier, full of self-importance and with a deep chest and combination of strength and activity, it makes an excellent family pet.

The double coat is pure white. The outer coat is formed of hard hair, about 5 cm (2 in) long and free from any curl, while the undercoat is short, soft and dense.

The West Highland White Terrier is a diminutive breed, with a height at the shoulder of about 27 cm (11 in). In weight it is 7.25–7.7 kg (16–17 lb).

*The Wire-haired Fox Terrier is alert and active.*

## Wire-haired Fox Terrier

This is an older breed than the Smooth-haired Fox Terrier and it can be traced back to the mid-18th century. They are alert, with quick movement and a 'tiptoe' stance, as if always expecting to be called into action.

It is a breed that is often clipped, although to many admirers the rough and countrified unclipped dog has much more appeal than one that has been clipped and prepared for display at a show.

The coat has a 'broken' nature, with hairs twisting and forming a dense, wiry coat said to resemble coconut matting. The coat is so dense that even when parted the skin cannot be seen. White should predominate.

Height at the shoulder is about 38 cm (15 in); a dog weighs 8 kg (18 lb) and a bitch 7.2 kg (16 lb).

*The West Highland White Terrier, often known as a 'Westie'.*

# Gundogs

These are dogs which hunt, point and retrieve birds from land or from water. The term 'point' refers to a dog's instinct to point by stopping and directing its muzzle towards game. This indicates to the hunter the location of the quarry and enables a closer approach, so as to be within gun range.

Pointing breeds were originally used by hunters who 'netted' game; the dog would stop and 'set', enabling the hunter to throw a net over the game before it became flushed and moved away. Incidentally, some pointers are referred to as setters.

## Clumber Spaniel

A large spaniel which took its name from Clumber, the seat of the Duke of Newcastle in Nottingham, England, where the breed was known in 1790. It gained prominence in the mid-1800s and has continued to be admired. It is a gentle, loyal and affectionate breed and ideal as a family pet.

It is large, with a square and heavy appearance and thoughtful expression. Yet, for all its size, it is an active breed.

It has an abundant, close and silky coat, plain white with lemon markings, straight on the back and flanks, and well-feathered legs.

In weight, dogs are 24–31 kg (55–70 lb) and bitches 20–27 kg (45–60 lb). At the shoulder, the breed is 45 cm (18 in) high.

*The Clumber Spaniel is loyal and affectionate.*

*The Cocker Spaniel is superb as a family pet.*

## Cocker Spaniel

This is one of the most popular spaniels, especially as a family pet. They are active and alert and full of fun. They get their name from sporting work in finding and flushing out woodcock, being especially good in thick and near-inaccessible scrub.

The breed is seen in a wide range of colours, including blue or red roan, red, golden, black-and-tan, liver or part-coloured. The coat is flat and silky, and neither waved nor wiry. Parts of the coat are feathered, but not excessively. In weight, they are 11–12.7 kg (25–28 lb); dogs are 38–40 cm (15–16 in) at their shoulders, and bitches 35–38 cm (14–15 in).

## Curly-coated Retriever

A smart, distinctive, upstanding and strong breed, full of fun and courage and with a coat packed with curls. It is the tallest of the retriever breeds and one of the oldest British gundogs.

*The Curly-coated Retriever is a faithful family pet.*

Additionally, it is an excellent breed for retrieving game from water and, perhaps, the most amusing of dogs to work with and a splendid companion.

They can be slightly aloof when meeting strangers, but within the family they are loyal and affectionate. Because they were bred for athleticism and endurance as a gundog, they require plenty of exercise when kept as a family pet.

There are two forms – black and liver (red). Both have plenty of eye-appeal, but the black type is the one that is most often seen.

In height, dogs are 63–68 cm (25–27 in) at the shoulder, and bitches are 58–63 cm (23–25 in). Weight is 31–36 kg (70–80 lb).

## English Setter

A handsome and long-established 'setting' breed, popular throughout the USA and the British Isles. The breed was originated to 'set' or 'point' upland game birds.

The coat is black-and-white, lemon-and-white, liver-and-white or tri-coloured (black, white and tan). They are flecked all over, but without large patches of colour. The coat is flat with variable length and light feathering.

It is docile and friendly and an ideal family pet.

It is a large breed, with a height to the shoulder of 63–68 cm (25–27 in) for dogs and 60–63 cm (24–25 in) for bitches. Dogs weigh 27–30 kg (60–66 lb) and bitches 25–28 kg (56-62 lb).

*The English Setter can be mischievous when young.*

## English Springer Spaniel

A long-established sporting gundog for flushing game into the air. Nowadays, they are frequently used by police and security organizations as sniffer dogs to detect illicit drugs, money, weapons and explosives. Some have also been trained to detect specific illnesses in humans.

They are happy, compact, strong and active, bred for endurance. As a family pet, this spaniel is affectionate and excitable, with a gentle disposition and a friendly, wagging tail. They like to please everyone.

Their coat is close, straight and weather-resistant, without being coarse. They are seen in many colours, but liver-and-white and black-and-white are the most usual. However, other colour medleys are known, including tan markings.

Height at the shoulder is about 50 cm (20 in), and they weigh 20–23 kg (45–50 lb).

*The Flat-coated Retriever has a docile temperament.*

## Flat-coated Retriever

This dog originated from a cross between the Lesser Newfoundland and the Labrador Retriever. These were then crossed with both Setters and Pointers and by 1860 a dog similar to the Flat-coated Retriever of today had been produced. However, the final type was not achieved until 20 years later.

They love water and will often wade in it just for the joy of being wet! They will retrieve game on land or in water. Additionally, these dogs are fun, very companionable, loyal and ideal as a family pet.

They are seen in two distinct colours – black or liver. Their coat is dense and as flat as possible, although around the chest and legs the coat is slightly thicker and raised.

In height, they are about 58 cm (23 in) at the shoulder, and 25–34 kg (55–75 lb) in weight.

*The English Springer Spaniel has a friendly disposition.*

## Golden Retriever

This is one of the best-known retrievers, with a very soft mouth for retrieving game. It is a popular gundog, having the nature of retrievers and setters with the scenting ability of the Bloodhound. It is descended from the Flat-coated Retriever and was originally known as the 'Flat-coated Retriever, Golden'. It gained prominence and in 1911 the Golden Retriever Club was formed.

They are handsome animals, with a beautiful golden (sometimes cream) coat, and a trustworthy, loyal and friendly nature that makes them an ideal family dog.

Their coat can be wavy or flat, with good feathering and a dense, water-resistant undercoat.

In height they are 58 cm (23 in) at the shoulder, and they weigh 29.5–31 kg (65–70 lb).

*The Gordon Setter was popular during the Victorian period.*

*Golden Retrievers are obedient and loyal family pets.*

## Gordon Setter

A distinguished and stylish setter, with a fearless, alert and intelligent nature. They were first heard of at Gordon Castle, Banffshire, Scotland, and named after Alexander, the fourth Duke of Gordon.

They have a deep-shining, coal-black coat with distinctive rich chestnut-red or mahogany markings. The head and front of the legs have a short but fine coat, but on other parts it is moderately long, fairly flat and relatively free from curl or wave. There is feathering on the upper parts of ears, backs of the hind legs and on the belly area.

Both puppies and adults can be boisterous and not always suited to homes with young children. The breed is slow to mature and needs to be trained from an early age.

Dogs are about 66 cm (26 in) at the shoulder, and bitches 60 cm (24 in). In weight, dogs are 29.5 kg (65 lb) and bitches 25.5 kg (56 lb).

*The Irish Setter is highly active and requires plenty of exercise to keep it healthy.*

## Irish Setter

Sometimes known as an Irish Red Setter and Red Setter, they are full of character and grace and probably the best known of all setters. They delight in a good gallop, every day!

They have a rich chestnut-coloured coat, without any trace of black. However, there is often white on the chest, throat or toes, or even a small star on the forehead.

The head, front of the legs and tips of the ears should have a fine and short coat, but on other parts, such as the legs and body, it should be moderately long and free from wave and curl. There is feathering on the upper parts of the ears.

In height they are about 63 cm (25 in) at the shoulder, and they weigh 29.5 kg (65 lb).

## Irish Water Spaniel

Sometimes known as the Rat Tail Spaniel and Shannon Spaniel, this is one of the largest and oldest spaniels and was developed in Ireland in the 1830s. It is an eager and intelligent gundog for work in boggy and wet areas. Indeed, the breed has been known as the Bog Dog.

They have a pleasant disposition, sometimes playing the mischievous clown and making an ideal family pet. It is not an aggressive breed but can make an ideal family guard dog.

The coat is formed of dense, tight and crisp ringlets, free from woolliness. In colour they are a rich, dark liver, with a purplish tint or bloom.

Height at the shoulder is 55–60 cm (22–24 in), and they weigh 25–27 kg (55–60 lb).

*The Irish Water Spaniel has a fun-loving nature.*

*Labrador Retrievers are always popular. Here are the three types (left to right): chocolate, yellow and black.*

## Labrador Retriever

Contrary to popular belief, this world-famous breed originated on the island of Newfoundland, not in the area then known as Labrador. The ancestry of the Labrador Retriever breed includes the St John's Water Dog.

Originally used by fishermen in the St John's area of Newfoundland to carry ropes between boats and to retrieve nets in the water, examples of the breed arrived in Britain in the early 1820s.

Few breeds are held in such high esteem as the Labrador Retriever – it repeatedly heads the Kennel Club's list of popular breeds. They are loyal and affectionate, without any hint of aggression, and therefore a superb family dog. They love to swim and be involved in catch-and-chase ball games.

The Labrador Retriever is strongly built, with a deep chest, and highly active, especially when young. Its coat is short and dense, smooth and without any wave. The undercoat is weather-resistant.

This breed is usually seen in black, but there are chocolate and yellow forms. The yellow type varies in colour from red to fawn.

This is a solid-bodied breed, with dogs weighing about (65 lb) and bitches slightly less. The height of a dog at the shoulder is 55–60 cm (22–24 in), bitches slightly less.

*There are several breeds of pointers; they are alert and direct their attention to the 'game'.*

## Pointer

This handsome and clean-cut gundog is known throughout
the world. It has a short, hard coat that is coloured lemon-
and-white, orange-and-white, liver-and-white, or black-and-
white. Sometimes, it is seen in just one colour.

The name derives from the dog's stance, with head and tail
stretched out when scenting game. Pointers are obedient and
require plenty of exercise.

They are about 60 cm (24 in) high at the shoulder, and
weigh 23–25 kg (50–55 lb).

## Sussex Spaniel

An English gundog, known more than two centuries ago
and developed in Sussex in southern England. It is a strong,
muscular, low and large, short-legged flusher of game, well
suited to activity in woodland scrub and among thick hedges.
They sometimes have a clownish and energetic temperament.

The Sussex Spaniel's coat is abundant, flat and with
no tendency to curl. However, the legs and rear are well
feathered. The colour is a rich golden-liver.

In height, the breed is 33–40 cm (13–16 in) at the shoulder,
and it weighs 15–20 kg (35–45 lb).

*The Sussex Spaniel often has a serious expression.*

# Pastoral breeds

There is a wide range of herding dogs throughout the world to suit differing climates and terrains. Some breeds act both as shepherds and guard dogs. Pastoral dogs are full of character, often a result of their close relationship with shepherds and the animals being herded. Many of these breeds are ideal as family dogs.

## Australian Heeler

Also known as the Australian Cattle Dog, Queensland Heeler and Hall's Heeler, its development is relatively recent and includes the old blue-merle coloured Collie, which was taken to Australia by Scottish farmers. Also in its lineage are the Kelpie (Australian Sheepdog) and Australian Wild Dog (Dingo).

The breed works silently and is very active, with amazing mobility and determination; it controls cattle in much the same way as the Welsh Corgi, by nipping at heels.

It has a longish head, tapering towards the jaws. The short, rather harsh-textured coat is usually red- or blue-speckled, but red-and-tan and red-and-white forms are known.

This breed weighs about 15 kg (35 lb) and is 50 cm (20 in) high at the shoulder.

*These Briard puppies will grow into large dogs.*

## Briard

Often known as the French Sheepdog, it has a long ancestry that can be traced to before the 12th century. It is also known as Chien de Berger de Brie. Napoleon Bonaparte is said to have admired this breed and had several on Corsica.

There are two forms of the Briard: the Smooth-haired and the Woolly-haired (the most popular type). The coat is medium to long, slightly undulating but not curled. Distinctively, hair on the head falls over the eyes in a shaggy forelock; the muzzle is often bearded and with a moustache.

The colour range is wide (except white). Popular colours are all-black, black with grey tips to the hairs, dark grizzle, and a range of browns. Some are fawn, silver-fawn or silver-grey.

It is a large breed and dogs are 60–68 cm (24–27 in) high at the shoulder, bitches 55–63 cm (22–25 in). In weight they are about 29.5 kg (65 lb).

*The Australian Heeler is an Australian working dog.*

# Collie

Also known as the Rough-coated Collie and Rough Collie, this is probably the best-known sheepdog and frequently seen in sheepdog trials, where its alertness, responsiveness to commands and general intelligence are soon apparent. It is an old breed and the working Collie can be traced back several hundred years.

The breed's name derives from the earlier named Colley Dog, which itself was gained from native mountain sheep called colleys and tended by farmers in the Scottish Highlands. The name Colley Dog, as well as Scotch Collie, are now only distant memories.

The Collie is alert, full of activity and strength of purpose, a quality especially needed when dealing with obstinate and disgruntled sheep.

The coat is a noticeable feature, profuse and dense, especially on the neck, back and tail. The outer coat is harsh and dense, while the undercoat is furry and soft; the mane is abundantly clothed in long hair. The coat's colour is usually sable, black-and-tan or blue-merle, with white blazes running up the forehead and often with a white throat and chest.

Dogs weigh 25–27 kg (55–60 lb) and bitches about 23 kg (50 lb). In height, dogs are about 60 cm (24 in) at the shoulder, and bitches 55 cm (22 in).

*The Long-haired Collie is often featured in 'movies'.*

*The Bearded Collie has a happy and fun-packed disposition.*

● **The Smooth-coated Collie** has a clean-cut outline, often appearing to have a longer body than the Rough-coated type because of the absence of a frilly main. In general, the hair itself is shorter than in the Rough-coated Collie (described above left), harsher in texture and lying close and flat to the body. The colour range is the same as that seen in the Rough-coated Collie.

● **The Bearded Collie** is a much different breed from either the Rough or Smooth types of collie and in many ways has more resemblance to the Old English Sheepdog (see page 65); both are claimed to have a related ancestry. Its history is long and has enabled it to collect several common names, including Highland Collie, Mountain Collie and Hairy Mou'ed Collie.

This breed is increasingly popular. Fifty or so years ago the best examples were to be found working flocks of sheep in Scotland, but now many families have appreciated the remarkable qualities of this breed – full of fun and with an agreeable character.

Its outer coat is shaggy and harsh, the undercoat soft and furry. The coat is abundant all over the body, including the head and legs, and extends down the legs as well as over the eyes and ears. The colour is usually slate or reddish-fawn, although some are shades of grey, brown and sandy – as well as black. White is usually abundant on the chest and front of the legs, as well as on parts of the face.

*The German Shepherd Dog has long been known in Europe.*

## German Shepherd Dog

This is the sheepdog of Germany and erroneously known, mainly in Britain, as the Alsatian. It is a very intelligent breed, characteristically with an expression of perpetual vigilance, liveliness and watchfulness, always alert to any sound or sight. The breed is also said to have the ability to reason when confronted with a problem.

It has been used to control sheep, cattle, pigs and goats and is claimed to have been known in the Early Bronze Age, some 6,000 years ago.

The breed is well proportioned, full of suppleness and plenty of muscle and endurance. The coat is smooth, at the same time being double-coated; the outer one is close and lying flat, and the undercoat is woolly, thick and close to the body. The colour range is wide and includes sable, brindle, grey, and black-and-tan.

In height, dogs are 60–66 cm (24–26 in) at the shoulder, and bitches 55–60 cm (22–24 in); in weight they are usually about 28 kg (62 lb).

## Old English Sheepdog

Often known as the Bob-tailed Sheepdog, there is no clear indication how this distinctive breed gained the 'Old' in its name. An early type of this breed is claimed to have been featured in a 1771 painting by Thomas Gainsborough, the English portrait and landscape painter. There are suggestions of a Russian heritage from the Owtcharka, and help from the Bearded Collie refined and produced the breed we know today as the Old English Sheepdog.

It was exhibited in an English dog show in 1873 under the name Shepherd Dog and taken to North America in the 1880s, where it became widely popular.

The Old English Sheepdog is unforgettable, resembling a bale of tasselled hay on four hairy legs! It has a distinctive walk, said to resemble, from a rear viewpoint, a bear's roll-like saunter. In earlier years, the tail was docked but such amputation is now illegal and the animal is able to swish its well-feathered tail.

Its coat is long, profuse, thick and shaggy, hanging down from the head and covering the ears and face. The body and legs are also well covered. In colour, the breed is usually any shade of grey, grizzle, blue or merle; mostly, the head, chest and front of the legs are white.

In height, dogs are 55–58 cm (22–23 in) at the shoulder, slightly less for bitches. Weight is 22–27 kg (50–60 lb).

*The Old English Sheepdog has a determined expression.*

## Rottweiler

This sturdy breed takes its name from the town of Rottweil in southern Germany, where its ancestors (possibly the now extinct Saufanger and Hatzrude) were used by Swabian knights to hunt wild boar. When the hunting of boars decreased, the breed became established as a cattle dog and, later, used by the police and army as a guard and defence dog.

It is muscular and broad, with a deep chest and legs set wide apart. The coat is short and smooth, black with distinct rich mahogany markings on the muzzle, cheeks, chest and legs. Usually, there is a tan spot over each eye.

In height, dogs are about 60–68 cm (24–27 in) at the shoulder, bitches 55–63 cm (22–25 in). In weight, dogs are 50–59 kg (110–130 lb), bitches 40–50 kg (88–110 lb).

*Rottweilers are courageous, self-assured and calm.*

*The Pyrenean Mountain Dog is exceptionally large and heavy.*

## Pyrenean Mountain Dog

For many centuries this large dog was known as Chien de Montagne des Pyrenees and, in North America, as the Great Pyrenees. There is also a Pyrenean Sheepdog, smaller and nimbler, which has taken over herding responsibilities from the Pyrenean Mountain Dog within the last hundred years.

The Pyrenean Mountain Dog is large and majestic, with a long, thick, flat outer coat formed of coarse hair, straight or slightly undulating; the undercoat is fine. The coat is all white or chiefly white, with markings of badger, grey or varying shades of tan.

Dogs are 68–82 cm (27–32 in) high at the shoulder, bitches 63–73 cm (25–29 in). In weight, dogs are 45–56 kg (100–125 lb) and bitches 40–52 kg (90–115 lb).

*Welsh Corgis are popular family pets, but can be snappy.*

# Welsh Corgi

There are two distinct varieties of this breed: the Pembrokeshire Welsh Corgi (better known) and the Cardiganshire Welsh Corgi. The Welsh Corgi dates back to the early 15th century when it was used as a droving dog to take black Welsh cattle to markets as far away as London. Apparently, drovers had the cattle shod to enable them to cope with rough roads. These cattle dogs ensured the stock would not wander off at night from pastures alongside the road, as well as lining up cattle with their heads close to the road's side when a stagecoach was due to pass. They also offered protection from highwaymen. The Cardiganshire Welsh Corgi is the type still used to control cattle, and the Pembrokeshire Corgi became smartened up for use as a family pet.

• **The Cardiganshire Welsh Corgi** has a distinctive 'foxy' appearance to its face that shows concentrated alertness. The coat is short or medium, with a hard texture, and any colour except white. In height the breed should be 30 cm (12 in) at the shoulder, with dogs weighing 10–12 kg (22–26 lb) and bitches 9–11 kg (20–24 lb).

• **The Pembrokeshire Corgi** has a 'foxy' face and expression, full of alertness and intelligence. The colour range is wider than in the Cardigan form, in single colours such as red, sable, fawn, and black-and-tan, or with white markings on the legs, chest and neck. At the shoulder, height is 25–30 cm (10–12 in). Dogs weigh 9–11 kg (20–24 lb), bitches 8–10 kg (18–22 lb).

# Welsh Springer Spaniel

Sometimes known as the Welsh Spaniel or Welsh Springer, in Wales it was earlier known as Welsh Starter from its ability to spring game into the air, usually for hunters using falcons. This breed is said to be the only spaniel native to Wales and descended from a race mentioned in the Ancient Laws of Wales and codified by Hywel Dda, some 1,000 years ago.

It is a compact and solidly built dog, ideal for hard work and endurance, with a body that, at first sight, appears to be too long; this is due to the angled forequarter and well-developed hindquarters.

It is handsome, loyal, conscientious and affectionate, often forming close associations with family members. This breed, however, is often wary of strangers until they are accepted into a family circle.

The coat is straight or flat, with a silky texture that is never wiry or waved. It should feel thick and weather-resistant. The coat colour is a medley of dark rich red and white.

In height, dogs are 45–48 cm (18–19 in) at the shoulder and bitches 43–45 cm (17–18 in). Weight is 15–20 kg (35–45 lb).

*The Welsh Springer Spaniel is alert to any movement.*

# Miniature and toy breeds

Toy and miniature dogs are popular family dogs, especially when there is a need for a small companion animal. They have just as much character and vitality as larger breeds, and as much sense and fortitude. Indeed, to a burglar a snappy and noisy small dog can be a greater deterrent than a large breed. There is a wide range of breeds to consider and many of them are described here.

## Affenpinscher

A German breed, related to the Miniature Pinscher and Griffon Bruxellois, with a proud, somewhat haughty but certainly intelligent nature. They were known in Europe in the 17th century, and the name Affenpinscher in German means 'monkey terrier'.

*The Affenpinscher was developed to control vermin.*

They are an excellent small guard dog, with a sharp bark and the courage of a lion. Additionally, they have the character of a terrier and will give chase to most things. Firm and early training is essential.

It is the nature of their coat that gives them their 'monkey-like' name. It is short and dense in some parts, and shaggy and much longer in others. Around the eyes, nose and chin, as well as on the legs, the coat is most shaggy.

The coat colour is usually black with tan markings, although blue, red or grey forms are occasionally seen.

In height at the shoulder the breed is about 25 cm (10 in), and it weighs approximately 2.7 kg (6 lb).

## Cavalier King Charles Spaniel

An active breed, full of fun and closely associated with the King Charles Spaniel. It has a relatively long and tapering muzzle, with questioning and appealing eyes that have made the breed popular as pets.

In earlier years, when King Charles Spaniels were being selected for breeding, it became fashionable to produce dogs with relatively short muzzles. Later, in the 1930s, a group of dedicated breeders decided to reintroduce the earlier and 'true' King Charles Spaniels; to ensure these new introductions could be easily identified from King Charles Spaniels they called them Cavalier King Charles Spaniels.

Unfortunately, this breed has suffered from inbreeding and up to 33% of them have Syringomyelia (a very painful condition). Additionally, about 50% suffer from heart disease.

Similar to the King Charles Spaniel, there are four different colour patterns (see page 72).

Cavalier King Charles Spaniels weigh slightly more than the King Charles Spaniel and are 4.5–6.3 kg (10–14 lb). Also, they are slightly higher at the shoulder at 30 cm (12 in).

*Chihuahuas are vivacious, happy and inquisitive family pets.*

## Chihuahua

One of the smallest dogs in the world, dainty, alert and with a saucy expression. It is native to Mexico and said to be partly derived from a small, Mexican temple dog which was known at the time of the Spanish invasion of Mexico in 1518. This native dog was recorded as then living wild in the mountains of Mexico, eating small rodents, young birds and other food.

Chihuahuas are excellent family dogs for small homes and flats, being playful and ideal watchdogs. There are two varieties – the smooth-coated (the most popular type in Britain) and the long-coated. Although they like warmth, they love to scamper outside during warm, dry weather.

They can be in any colour or mixture of colours, including white, black and tan. Both dogs and bitches weigh under 2.7 kg (6 lb), and in height at the shoulder are usually 15-23 cm (6-9 in). However, sometimes they are taller, at 30 cm (12 in).

*Cavalier King Charles Spaniels are highly attentive.*

## Griffon

A distinctive, perky, alert, obedient and lively Belgium dog, first exhibited in Brussels in 1880. There are two forms of it – the rough-coated (Griffon Bruxellois) and the smooth-coated (Petit Brabanon); both are usually classified as Griffon. Their ancestry can be traced back to the 15th century; one is pictured in a painting of that time by the Flemish artist Jan van Eyck (c.1395–c.1441) called 'Giovanni Arnolfini and His Bride'.

This breed is easily trained, excelling in obedience tests, and makes an ideal family pet. The rough-coated type has a harsh and wiry coat, free from curl, while the smooth type is short and smooth. The range of colour is wide and includes clear-red, black, or black-and-rich-tan.

They vary in size, from 1.36 to 4.5 kg (3–10 lb), but are most desirable at 2.7–4 kg (6–9 lb). In height, they should not be above 27 cm (11 in).

*The Chinese Crested Dog is rare and distinctive.*

## Chinese Crested Dog

Hairless dogs are among the rarest of breeds and, without doubt, the most bizarre. The head of the Chinese Crested Dog (sometimes just known as the Chinese Crested) carries a crest of flowing hair; there is also hair on the feet and a plume on the end of the tail. The rest of the dog is naked. The skin is fine and silky to touch, varying in colour and usually mottled, like bark on a plane tree.

The reasons for this hairlessness are not fully understood, but in practical terms such animals need protection from strong sunlight and extremes of temperature. However, they have the advantage of not having a body odour, not shedding of hair and, of course, being free from fleas!

*The Griffon demonstrates self-importance and authority.*

*Italian Greyhounds have appealed to royalty and painters.*

## Italian Greyhound

A delightful, high-stepping, lively and affectionate miniature greyhound, claimed to have been introduced into Britain in the Tudor period (1485–1603). However, as the name indicates, it comes from Italy and is known as Piccola Lavriere Italiana. Its lineage goes back a long way and the breed can claim to have been a favourite with Roman, Greek and Egyptian nobility. Additionally, these dogs have been a favourite with both painters and royalty, including Charles I, Frederick the Great and Queen Victoria.

Their skin is fine and supple, with a thin and glossy coat, resembling satin. There are several colours – shades of fawn, fawn-and-white, cream, blue, black-and-fawn, and white-pied. In height they are 25 cm (10 in) at the shoulder and in weight 2.7–3.6 kg (6–8 lb).

## Japanese Spaniel

Also known as the Japanese Chin, this is a lively, high-spirited, happy and intelligent ancient breed, known in China some 2,500 years ago and arriving in Japan about 1,000 years later. They resemble Pekingese and became favourites of Japanese royalty.

They are thought to have cat-like traits, having great agility and preferring to rest on high surfaces, such as the backs of sofas and chairs. Usually they are quiet, but they will bark at the presence of a visitor.

In colour they are usually either black-and-white or red-and-white. Some forms, however, have a mixture of colours including shades of sable, brindle, lemon and orange.

In height they are 20–27 cm (8–11 in) at the shoulder, and they weigh 3–4 kg (7–9 lb).

*Japanese Spaniels rarely bark and are not 'yappy'.*

## King Charles Spaniel

Popularized by Charles II, it is thought that this breed was developed by crossing short-nosed breeds from China with Maltese dogs. However, dogs with a likeness to King Charles Spaniels were known back in the time of King Henry VIII (1491–1547) and mentioned by Queen Elizabeth I's physician. King Charles I owned one, but it was his son who made them better known.

They were more or less banned at the English Court after the fall of the Stuarts in 1714 (on the death of Queen Anne) but, fortunately, they were kept in many country houses. During the Victorian era they regained popularity when a King Charles Spaniel named Dash was a play companion for royal children.

They are often bumptious, but always full of fun, with deep and wide chests. Distinctively, their ears are set low and hang flat to their cheeks. The coat is long and silky, with a slight wave but not curly, with ears, legs and tail well feathered.

The breed has four distinct colour patterns: ruby (totally rich chestnut-red); rich black with mahogany markings; tri-coloured in white, black and tan; and Blenheim (a ground colour of pearly-white, with chestnut-red patches).

In height they are about 25 cm (10 in) at the shoulder, and they average 4 kg (9 lb) in weight.

*The King Charles Spaniel is a widely favoured lapdog.*

*The Lhasa Apso is attractive and requires regular grooming.*

## Lhasa Apso

A distinctive Tibetan small breed (not a toy), similar to a Skye Terrier (see page 53), with a coat that is excessively long and shaggy. It is claimed that since the 16th century and until recent years it was presented by the Dalai Lama to neighbouring rulers.

It also resembles the Shih Tzu (see page 78), but with a much longer muzzle. Colour forms are honey, golden or sandy, and it is about 25 cm (10 in) high at the shoulder. In weight it ranges from 5.4 to 8 kg (12–18 lb).

*The Maltese is one of the earliest of all lapdogs.*

## Maltese

Sweet and highly intelligent, it is probably the oldest of all European toy dogs, with a heritage dating back 3,000 years, and it was a strong favourite with ladies of nobility in Rome and Greece.

Its body is short, cobby and low to the ground, with its back straight from the top of the shoulders to the tail. The coat is silky and long, straight and not woolly. They can be seen in any single colour, but not pure white.

In height at the shoulder dogs are 20–25 cm (8–10 in), bitches 17–22 cm (7–9 in). In weight, they are about 3 kg (7 lb).

## Miniature Bull Terrier

This highly intelligent dog very much resembles the normal Bull Terrier (see page 48), except that it is only 35 cm (14 in) high at the shoulder and weighs under 9 kg (20 lb).

This is an active breed; although small, it requires plenty of exercise each day.

## Miniature Long-haired Dachshund

Bright, active and bold, this miniature dog is highly intelligent and should be a small version of the larger counterpart (see page 41). The coat must be soft and straight, or only slightly waved. The weight must be no more than 5 kg (11 lb) and, preferably, 3–4 kg (7–9 lb).

*The Miniature Pinscher exudes vitality and fun.*

## Miniature Pinscher

An alert, elegant breed, full of spirit, with the Doberman Pinscher in its formation. These dogs are full of vitality and vigour and always ready to impress people. However, their natural aggression and overconfidence can make them difficult to train.

The coat is short and smooth and usually black-and-tan, tan, red, blue or fawn.

In height they are 25–30 cm (10–12 in) at the shoulder, and they weigh 3.6–4.5 kg (8–10 lb).

*The Miniature Poodle is amusing and fun-loving.*

## Miniature Poodle

These are similar to their larger and well-known counterparts, except in size. They are elegant, active and intelligent, with a height at the shoulder of 38 cm (15 in).

It was during the 1950s that this miniature breed became popular and, at first, many examples were nervous and neurotic. Fortunately, these characteristics have been bred out and now they are bright and active small dogs, well suited to living in a small house. They usually love to perform tricks in front of an audience.

Similarly to the standard-sized Poodle, miniature types also need clipping. It is possible to undertake this at home, but it is best undertaken professionally.

## Miniature Schnauzer

In the same manner as most miniature breeds, this one is a replica of the larger and standard-sized type (see page 85). However, despite a miniature size, they are just as active, with a height at the shoulder of 35 cm (14 in) for dogs and 32 cm (13 in) for bitches. They are full of character, being bold, intelligent and superb when undertaking obedience tests.

## Miniature Smooth-haired Dachshund

Similarly to the Miniature Long-haired Dachshund, this delightful dog should be a smaller version of its larger counterpart and not exceed 5 kg (11 lb). It is a miniature breed that is much admired, an ideal dog for a small home.

## Papillon

A toy spaniel, often known as the Butterfly Dog, that derives its name from the shape of its fringed ears which suggest an open-winged butterfly. Occasionally, it is known as the Squirrel Dog, in response to the way it carries its tail.

The breed is claimed to be of Chinese origin, with a small Chinese Spaniel and the Mexican Chihuahua in its parentage. Although small and a lapdog, it nevertheless delights in country walks and running through long grass.

Papillons are highly intelligent and ideal with children, strangers, and other animals.

It is a distinctive breed, with large ears, upright or dropped, and a long tail set high over its body. The coat is white, with patches of any colour. The long, soft and silky coat has additional frills on the chest, ears, back of the legs and the tail.

In height they are 20–28 cm (8–11 in) at the shoulder, and they weigh 2.2–4.5 kg (5–10 lb).

*The Papillon has beautiful butterfly-like ears.*

## Pekingese

An ancient breed dating back in China to around 2,000 years ago. They were introduced into England by soldiers who had looted the Imperial Palace in Peking (now Beijing) during the Boxer Rebellion in 1900.

These small dogs, often known as Lion Dogs, are alert, intelligent, fearless and adaptable, with great beauty and dignity. Additionally, they are full of fun and make ideal companions for people of all ages.

The head is relatively large and broad, and the body is short. The coat is long and straight, with a profuse mane extending beyond the shoulders and forming a cape-like veil at the sides of the face and around the neck. The coat colour is usually red, tri-coloured or parti-coloured.

In weight, dogs are 3–5 kg (7–11 lb) and bitches 3.6–5.4 kg (8–12 lb). At the shoulder, they are 15–23 cm (6–9 in) high.

*The Pomeranian has an amazingly thick coat.*

## Pomeranian

A miniature Spitz-type breed, with a massively upstanding coat, pricked ears and tail curled over its back.

The breed became popular in the 1870s and its fame was further enhanced when Queen Victoria kept one. It is an excellent breed for small houses and apartments, at the same time being active, intelligent and very obedient. However, they have to be trained early or they may try to impose their will on the household.

Like many other breeds, Pomeranians have two coats: an undercoat and an overcoat. The undercoat is soft and fluffy, while the upper one is long, perfectly straight, harsh in texture and covering the entire body. It is most abundant around the neck and forepart of the shoulders and chest.

Pomeranians have a range of colours, but with each animal showing just a single colour. These are usually orange or red, although others are seen and these include cream, black and chocolate.

In height, the breed is about 18 cm (7 in) at the shoulder. In weight dogs are 1.8–2 kg (4–4 lb) and bitches 2–2.4 kg (4–5 lb).

*The Pekingese can often be wilful and aloof.*

*The Pug is non-aggressive and good with children.*

## Pug

A delightful dog that is intelligent and eager to please owners and gives total allegiance. It is thought that Dutch traders from the Dutch East India Company introduced this breed from China to Britain in 1884. The breed became fashionable, especially with ladies of nobility.

Pugs have a cobby, square, muscular and compact appearance, with a fine and smooth, short and glossy coat, neither hard nor woolly. Characteristically, it has a short-muzzled face. Unfortunately, Pugs (as well as other breeds, including Pekingese, with flattened faces) suffer from breathing problems.

Colours are fawn, apricot-fawn, silver, brindle or black. The tail normally curls tightly over the animal's hip.

In weight, both dogs and bitches are 6–8 kg (14–18 lb).

## Schipperke

A small, cobby breed with a lively and sharp disposition. It is a tireless guard dog, an excellent ratter and a superb swimmer, and is used to protect barges and their goods. Indeed, the name Schipperke means 'little boatman'.

In temperament they are headstrong, stubborn and mischievous and sometimes known as Little Black Fox, Tasmanian Black Devil and Little Black Devil. Additionally, in many countries they are known as Belgian Ship Dogs and Belgian Barge Dogs.

It is a distinctive breed, having a double coat with a soft and fluffy undercoat and a harsher-textured outer one. A distinctive ruff surrounds the neck. The coat is black.

In height, the breed is about 30 cm (12 in) at the shoulder, and it weighs around 6.8 kg (15 lb).

*The Schipperke tends to be suspicious of strangers.*

## Shetland Sheepdog

Earlier known in the Outer Hebrides and the Orkneys as the Tounie Dog and Peerie Dog, this miniature sheepdog is now better known as a Sheltie or Shetland Collie. It is graceful, lithe, alert, intelligent and gentle and makes an ideal companion in a small home.

It is a miniature version of a Smooth-coated Collie (see page 64), with a double coat; the outer one is formed of long, harsh hair, while the undercoat is soft, short and close to the body. The mane and frill around the neck is full and abundant, with the forelegs well feathered.

There are several colours, such as tri-coloured (black with tan and white markings), black with white markings, sable, and merle (blue-grey mixture flecked or ticked with black).

Height at the shoulder is about 35 cm (14 in), and it weighs approximately 6.3 kg (14 lb).

*The Shetland Sheepdog has a docile temperament.*

*The Shih Tzu has an extrovert and vivacious personality.*

## Yorkshire Terrier

A perky, highly intelligent British breed of toy terrier and thought to have been a descendant of the old Black-and-Tan Terrier and Skye Terrier; formerly, it was used to catch rats in Yorkshire cotton mills. It is often known as 'Yorkie' and became fashionable towards the end of the 1800s, retaining popularity ever since.

These dogs have a compact and upright carriage which conveys their feeling of self-importance! The coat is straight, not wavy, glossy and like silk, with a fine texture. In colour it is dark steel-blue with tan shading.

It is about 20 cm (8 in) high at the shoulder and weighs about 3 kg (7 lb).

## Shih Tzu

A Chinese breed related to the Tibetan Lhasa Apso and the Pekingese; it increasingly became known in Britain in the 1930s. This small dog (it is not a toy type) is alert and active and claimed to have an arrogant carriage.

It is distinctive, with a broad and round head and widely spaced eyes. The head becomes cloaked in hair which falls over the eyes. Additionally, its beard and whiskers produce a chrysanthemum-like effect.

The coat is long and dense, but not curly, and seen in many colours, preferably with a white blaze on the forehead and a white tip to the tail.

Height at the shoulder is 25–27 cm (10–11 in), and it weighs in the region of 6.8 kg (15 lb).

*The Yorkshire Terrier has a lively and perky nature.*

# Utility breeds

Hounds, terriers, gun and pastoral dogs have qualities that have enabled them to become well known, whether in the control of vermin, herding animals, tracking or aiding in the detection and retrieving of birds. Some breeds, however, do not neatly fall into these groups, although many have their qualities. These utility breeds, sometimes known as service dogs, have been especially adapted through breeding for such diverse roles as guarding and defending property, fighting in bull-pits, and running alongside horse-drawn carriages. These are dogs that are full of character and many are excellent as family pets.

## Boxer

Bright, stocky, friendly, lithe and loyal, this distinctive breed originated in the 1890s in Germany from the now extinct Bullenbeisser, a mastiff-type, and the English Bulldog. The breed became known in many parts or Europe in the late 19th century and was introduced into North America at the turn of the century. It is said to have gained its name from a tendency to stand on its rear legs and appear to use its front paws like a boxer.

The Boxer has a boisterous, active and self-confident character and when faced with danger reveals outstanding bravery. Yet in a family situation it is friendly, playful and gentle with children. Because of its short coat, the Boxer does not live comfortably in extremes of cold or heat, but in temperate climates is a superb family pet.

The head is the most noticeable feature, with a wide and distinctive muzzle and the lower jaw protruding beyond the upper one. The coat is short and shiny, smooth and close and tight to the body. Popular colours include fawn and brindle, often with white on the feet and underbelly.

In height, dogs are 55–60 cm (22–24 in) at the shoulder, bitches slightly less at 53–58 cm (21–23 in). Dogs weigh about 30 kg (66 lb) and bitches 28 kg (62 lb).

*The Boxer has a lithe and supple body action.*

*The Bulldog has a pugnacious and stalwart nature.*

*The Bullmastiff makes a delightful and loyal companion.*

## Bulldog

A well-known British breed which evolved from larger, foreign short-faced dogs and originally bred for bull-baiting contests, until they become illegal in England in the 19th century.

This distinctive breed is characterized by a pugnacious appearance, broad shoulders and widely positioned legs. Their muscular, thick-set body has a finely textured, short, close and smooth coat. The colour – including brindle, fawn, red or white – is over the entire body; occasionally there are black muzzles or dark shading on the fore-face.

Height at the shoulder is about 38 cm (15 in), with dogs weighing 25 kg (55 lb) and bitches 22 kg (50 lb).

## Bullmastiff

A powerfully built breed with great strength and endurance combined with alertness, high spirits and reliability. It is an old British watchdog, but not confirmed as a breed until 1924. It was earlier known as the Keepers' Night Dog.

The face is large and Pug-like, handsome and alert. The chest is wide and deep, well set between the forelegs, with strong shoulders very much evident. The coat is short and hard, lying flat to the body. Coat colour can be any shade of brindle, fawn or red, but it must be pure and clear.

In height, dogs are 63–68 cm (25–27 in) at the shoulder, bitches 60–66 cm (24–26 in). In weight, dogs are 50–59 kg (110–130 lb), bitches 40–50 kg (90–110 lb).

*The Chow Chow has a lion-like appearance.*

## Chow Chow

Highly distinctive Chinese breed with a cobby, lion-like appearance and dignified, aloof bearing. Earlier it was bred for its fur and flesh, but is now kept as a family pet. It is unique in having a bluish-black tongue and stilted gait.

It is an active breed, with a compact body and tail carried backwards well over its back. The dense, abundant, straight coat stands off from the body; the outer coat is coarse, while the undercoat is soft and woolly. There are many colours, but they are entire and cover the complete body. They can be white, fawn, cream, blue, red or black.

At the shoulder the breed is about 45 cm (18 in) high, and it weighs 25–27 kg (55–60 lb).

# Dalmatian

Full of character and an ideal family dog, this breed always creates amusement. It has a long list of descriptive names, including Plum Pudding Dog, Firehouse Dog, Carriage Dog and Spotted Carriage Dog.

At one time, these dogs were considered to be unintelligent, but now it is known that they have a predisposition for deafness, which can cause problems.

A loyal, intelligent, playful and active dog, it was earlier used as a gundog on the West Balkans coast and later as a coach dog in Britain. Of course, the breed gained further fame when it was featured in the film 'One Hundred and One Dalmatians', based on the 1956 novel by the British author Dodie Smith.

Once seen, never forgotten, they have a short, dense and glossy white coat peppered with black or brown spots.

In height dogs are 53–63 cm (21–25 in) at the shoulder, bitches 45–60 cm (18–24 in). In weight, dogs are about 25 kg (55 lb) and bitches slightly less at 23 kg (50 lb).

*The Dobermann Pinscher is lithe, alert and intelligent.*

# Dobermann Pinscher

Alert, elegant and with an upright stance, this breed was developed in Germany in the 1890s by Herr Louis Dobermann, with a view to creating a dog with strength, speed, endurance, intelligence, ferocity and loyalty. At that time, Herr Dobermann was a tax collector and needed a dog for protection. Later developments by other dog breeders created the breed we know today. In German, the word *Pinscher* means terrier; later, this name was removed as through the dog's development the terrier part became diluted by the introduction of other breeds into its heritage. Nowadays, most people just refer to this breed as a Dobermann.

The coat is smooth, short-haired, hard, thick and close-lying against the body. In colour, it can be black, tan or dark blue, with rust-red markings, clearly defined and appearing above each eye, on the muzzle, throat and front of the chest.

Height for dogs is about 66 cm (26 in) at the shoulder, bitches 63 cm (25 in). It weighs around 28 kg (62 lb).

*The Dalmatian is a fun dog for the whole family.*

*The Great Dane has been called the 'Apollo of dogs'.*

## Great Dane

Large, elegant, intelligent and muscular European breed, earlier used for bear and boar hunting but now solely as a guard dog or family pet (if the house is large enough!). Where space allows, this is an affectionate and, with patience, trainable breed, but usually a 'one-person dog'.

Its silhouette is distinctive; neck and head are carried high (except when galloping) and it has a long back. Although large, it is lithe and remarkably agile, especially when young.

The coat is dense, short, sleek and usually fawn, brindle, blue, striped or black. It is tall and large, 75 cm (30 in) at the shoulder; dogs weigh 54 kg (120 lb), bitches 45 kg (100 lb).

*The Keeshond is intelligent and forever alert.*

## Keeshond

A native Dutch Spitz-type breed, which is associated with activities on canals, with a tail that curls over its body. They are alert, with a fox-like head and short, compact body. The coat is dense and stands outwards, with a dense ruff and well-feathered trousers. Additionally, they have a light, dense and soft undercoat.

The coat's colour is ash-grey, similar to a wolf, or tawny.

Height at the shoulder is 45 cm (18 in) for dogs, 43 cm (17 in) for bitches. The average weight is about 17 kg (38 lb).

*The Newfoundland has a friendly and easy-going nature.*

## Newfoundland

Widely famed breed used in its native Newfoundland as a rescuer of fishermen and retriever of nets. During the fishing season it was also used to haul fishermen's carts laden with cod and fishing equipment, and in winter it pulled carts full of fuel from local forests.

This is a gentle and docile breed, with a broad and deep head held high and a short, powerful neck. The fairly coarse and oily, dull jet-black coat is dense and lies flat to the body.

The Landseer Newfoundland breed, which was made popular by the 19th-century English painter Sir Edwin Landseer, is black-and-white.

This is a large and stocky breed, about 73 cm (29 in) at the shoulder for a dog, slightly less for a bitch. Dogs weigh 63–68 kg (140–150 lb), bitches 50–54 kg (110–120 lb).

*The Poodle has a bright and active attitude to life.*

## Poodle

Active, elegant, and said to be the most intelligent breed after the Collie and before the German Shepherd Dog. It is thought to have originated in Germany about 400 years ago, with the English word 'poodle' derived from the Low German word *pudel* or *puddeln*, meaning to splash in water. This is an indication of the breed's earlier use as a gundog and retriever of game from water. Additionally, it was employed to search for truffles.

The coat is hard-textured and profuse, with close curls – thick without knots. There are several colours – entirely black, white, brown, or blue. White Poodles have dark eyes, black noses, lips and toenails. Brown Poodles have dark-amber eyes, dark-liver noses, lips and toenails. Blue Poodles have dark eyes, lips and toenails. Black Poodles are especially handsome, with dark eyes, black noses, lips and toenails.

Usually, Poodles are clipped and this is something best left to Poodle-clipping experts. However, to many people they appear just as attractive with the coat growing naturally.

Apart from the standard-sized Poodle, there are miniature forms (see page 74). The standard Poodle is over 38 cm (15 in) high at the shoulder. The weights of standard Poodles vary: dogs are 20–32 kg (45–70 lb), and bitches 20–27 kg (46–60 lb).

## Portuguese Water Dog

Also known as the Portuguese Diving Dog, Portuguese Fishing Dog and Cão de Água, this extraordinary swimmer and diver was used by Portuguese fisherfolk as early as the 14th century. It was used to dive to retrieve breaking nets and to catch fish which had escaped or fallen out of nets. It was also employed as a courier between boats, with messages in cylinders attached around the dog's neck.

The coat is profuse and formed of strong hair, except where clipped from around the back legs and lower abdomen. Colours are black, black-and-white, rusty dark grey, rusty dark grey, brown, brown-and-white, and white.

There is also a Curly-coated Portuguese Water Dog, with a short coat formed of tight, cylindrical curls, resembling those of an Irish Water Spaniel.

Height at the shoulder for dogs is about 53 cm (21 in), and slightly less for bitches. Dogs weight about 20 kg (45 lb), and bitches approximately 18 kg (40 lb).

*The Portuguese Water Dog possesses a friendly disposition.*

*The Saint Bernard is a life-saving Alpine breed.*

## Samoyed

Intelligent, alert and active breed, earlier used as a herding, hunting and general-purpose dog by the Samoyed tribe on the northern edge of the Siberian Plain.

A distinctively Spitz-type dog, with a body well covered with a thick, close, soft and short undercoat, and harsh hair growing through it and forming an outer coat which stands out from the body. The tail is long and profuse; when the animal is alert, it is carried over the body, but it droops when the dog is at rest.

The breed is seen in several different colours – pure white, cream, or biscuit-and-white.

In height, dogs are 50–55 cm (20–22 in) at the shoulder, bitches 45–50 cm (18–20 in). In weight, dogs are 20–25 kg (45–55 lb), bitches 16–20 kg (36–45 lb).

## Saint Bernard

Few breeds are as legendary as this large bundle of mountain rescue. The Swiss enjoy a long tradition of rescue work in the Alps using this breed; it was similarly used in the Himalayas.

A large breed, with a muscular and broad body and face that portrays dignity, intelligence and benevolence. There are two differently coated types of Saint Bernard. In the Smooth-coated form the coat is set close to the body and hound-like, with slight feathering on the tail and thighs. The Rough-coated type has a dense and flat coat, rather fuller around the neck.

The coat's colour encompasses orange, mahogany-brindle and red-brindle, with white patches on the body. Additionally, the muzzle is white and there is a white blaze on the face. The neck, collar, chest, forelegs and feet have white patches, as does the end of the tail. There are black shadings on the ears and face.

Height to the shoulder is about 71 cm (28 in), and it weighs 81–90 kg (180–200 lb).

*The Samoyed is friendly, alert and intelligent.*

*The Schnauzer is active, alert and inquisitive.*

## Schnauzer

An old German dog, thought to have originated in the 15th and 16th centuries. It gained its name from the German word for 'snout', referring to the dog's distinctively bearded snout. Although considered to be a terrier-type breed, the Schnauzer is calmer and less energetic, making it easier to train. They are loyal companions and rarely aggressive to strangers, unless provoked. They have been used in many ways, to catch rats, as police dogs and to carry messages on battle fronts during times of war.

There are three forms of this breed, the 'standard' (the one that is discussed here), the 'giant' (often 60 cm/24 in at the shoulder and weighing 25–36 kg/55–80 lb) and the 'miniature' (see page 74).

Incidentally, Giant Schnauzers were earlier used as working dogs, herding cattle and guarding premises.

In general appearance, the Schnauzer is robust, sinewy and nearly square (the length of the body being equal to the height). Its coat is wiry and hardy, smart and neat. In colour it is pure black or iron- or steel-grey.

In height, dogs are about 48 cm (19 in) at the shoulder, and bitches 45 cm (18 in). They weigh about 17 kg (38 lb).

## Weimaraner

An alert and attractive breed originating in Germany and also known as the Weimaraner Vorstehhund and Grey Ghost. It has been used to track and retrieve game, and its alert and disciplined nature has made it ideal as a police dog. It has also been employed in the armed forces.

The coat is smooth and sleek, in shades of silver, mouse or roe-grey, blending into a lighter shade around the head.

In height, dogs are 58–63 cm (23–25 in) at the shoulder, bitches 56–60 cm (22–24 in). In weight, dogs are 25–30 kg (55–65 lb), bitches 20–25 kg (45–55 lb).

*The Weimaraner is a friendly and protective family dog.*

# INTRODUCING A PUPPY INTO YOUR HOME

# Welcoming your new puppy and helping him settle in

The way a new puppy or dog is welcomed and introduced into a home is important as it sets the scene for the rest of the animal's life. It is also essential that you are prepared with drinking and feeding containers (see page 89), as well as both a day and a night bed (see pages 93–94).

*A new life with a new family is an exciting and major happening in a young pup's life.*

## Puppy pens and boxes

In a pup's early weeks with you it is wise to constrain him to specific areas in your house and, preferably, in something like a child's play-pen. Usually, a surround of stiff, close-mesh, plastic-covered wire-netting needs to be fixed to its inside to prevent him squeezing out. However, special pens are available for constraining puppies. These can be bought, or your vet may have some to loan.

Large cardboard boxes are another solution and these can be easily cut and adapted by the use of a scalpel or sharp knife; use strong and wide brown tape to secure the sides and edges.

Cover the floor with a plastic sheet, then put several sheets of newspaper on top.

### Feeding a puppy and early toilet training

These are important aspects of a puppy's life and they are described elsewhere in this book:

★ **Feeding a puppy** – see pages 138–141.

★ **Early toilet training** – see pages 110–111.

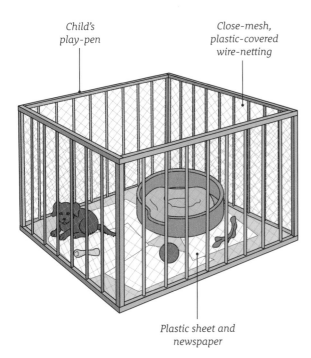

Child's
play-pen

Close-mesh,
plastic-covered
wire-netting

Plastic sheet and
newspaper

*Young puppies need to be safeguarded from dangers in a new
home, as well as from their own puppy silliness.*

## Keeping your puppy calm

The excitement a family generates when receiving a puppy
into their home can be overwhelming for a pup. Therefore,
remember that his immediate requirements are food and
water, together with sleep and privacy. He needs his own
territory, where he feels secure from the bustle of family life.

Privacy at this stage in a pup's life helps to reduce the chance
of him becoming neurotic in later years, perhaps barking
excessively, howling and gnawing his own nails and paws.

Do not underestimate the value of giving a puppy quiet times
to himself – there will be many other opportunities to have
fun with him.

These quiet a[...]
from strong and [...]
Conservatories are [...]
that he is not in stro[...]
during hot weather ca[...]
high for a puppy.

### Food and water bowl[...]

These are essential and must su[...]

★ Puppies require bowls with shallo[...]
which they can safely lean to reach foo[...]
without toppling over and falling in.

★ As puppies grow, they can be given larger a[...]
stronger bowls, which cannot be pushed aroun[...]
floor through enthusiastic eating. Heavy stonewa[...]
types are best for large and heavy breeds, while me[...]
and plastic ones suit small and light types, or when [...]
the animal is young.

★ Placing a large plastic mat under the bowls helps to
keep the floor clean; choose smooth-surfaced types as
they can be easily washed and wiped dry.

★ Newspapers are ideal for spreading over the feeding
area, especially when puppies are young.

★ All feeding and drinking bowls must be thoroughly
cleaned each day to prevent contamination from food
left to dry on them.

★ Fresh water is essential, so you must replace the
water in the bowl at least once a day.

*...her and siblings.*

...eas should be slightly wa...
direct heat) and free fro...
...suitable places, but in s...
...g and direct sunlight; te...
...like those in a car, be ...

...t the size of the dog.
...y sides, over
...d or water

...s away from
...e will not have the
...s and sisters. Even if settled in
...pen, he will express his apprehension at
... alone. But do not be tempted to take him into your
...edroom and onto your bed. Later, you may have his night bed, perhaps a traditional wickerwork dog basket, in your bedroom, but for now he should remain in his own, private area. Say goodnight to him and leave.

When you come down in the morning, make a fuss of him and say what a good boy he has been. He will soon learn the nightly routine and accept it.

## Bones and 'treats'

A young puppy delights in a large, raw, beef shin bone. This is a natural way for a pup to clean his teeth; it also helps him to shed his milk teeth. Additionally, it provides calcium and exercise for the pup's jaws. However, do not give a pup or (later) a dog small bones or those that splinter.

Alternatively, instead of giving a pup a bone, provide him with a 'chewy treat' specially sold for puppies; they are less hazardous than a bone and often recommended by vets. A chewy treat often becomes a pup's prized possession.

### Puppy toys

Similarly to adult dogs, puppies like to have a toy of their own – but ensure it is safe and will not break or be small enough to lodge in its throat.

Take care not to provide a pup too early with an old slipper, as this might provide encouragement for him to chew ones still in use. In later years, when a pup reaches adulthood, discarding an old slipper at Christmas to a dog that, from experience, is knowingly awaiting it is one of the amusing and simple pleasures of having a family dog.

*Puppies love to chew – but avoid giving them bones or sticks that splinter and wedge in their teeth and throats.*

*Puppies need to be kept secure and safe during their early weeks and months with you.*

## Puppy beds

The range of beds for puppies is wide:

• A strong cardboard box forms an ideal temporary bed as it can be inexpensively replaced if soiled. A sharp knife or scalpel can soon shape the box, creating a draught-proof back and sides, as well as a low and easily accessible front.

• Circular, rigid, plastic types with high sides provide a draught-proof, waterproof and washable bed. Additionally, they are durable and relatively inexpensive.

• A home-made wooden box, raised about 5 cm (2 in) above the floor, is excellent. Ensure it is constructed from clean, non-chemical-impregnated or painted wood; puppies love to chew and soon absorb toxic chemicals from wood and preservative paints.

• Folding beds that later can be used for travelling and taking your dog on family holidays are useful.

• Wickerwork baskets are traditional homes for pups and dogs and can be bought in several sizes. Puppies – and dogs – are often tempted to chew the sides, especially at the front, but stout string can usually be used to make repairs. Do not use wire that may break and harm your pet.

### Dangerous bed for puppies

A large, squashy bean-bag is suitable and very comfortable for an older animal, but for a puppy can be dangerous as they naturally chew and may swallow pieces of the filling.

When older, a dog may appreciate this type of bed as it is adaptable to any shape and easily fits into a corner, which they often prefer.

## Types of bedding for a pup

Thin, mattress-like bedding for the base of a bed is available, but make sure it has a waterproof covering. Cover this with an old, soft blanket. The puppy will inspect it and may tug a blanket to one side to make it more personal and comfortable – but this is to be expected as it is his own, private area.

**Please note:** Some of these beds are also suitable when your pup grows into adulthood – but ensure it is large enough to enable the animal to spread out and go through its ritual of turning around several times before settling down.

*A wickerwork basket with a cushion provides a safe and comfortable home for your pet.*

### Accidents will happen

Puppies and dogs need dry, clean and comfortable bedding. When young, a plastic cover for the bed's base prevents it becoming soiled, but during a pup's early weeks expect to have a few accidents. Therefore:

★ Check his bedding every morning. Even if not soiled, it will need airing.

★ Wash all soiled bedding and dry and properly air it; your pup will not be comfortable on damp bedding.

★ Wash and replace bedding each week.

*Puppies are inquisitive and attracted to moving images on a television or computer.*

## Puppies and dogs on your own bed

Discourage this from the first moment he 'tries it on', for several reasons:

• All animals (including your puppy) carry diseases that could be troublesome to humans and are especially contractible if in close proximity with you at night.

• Fleas, an ongoing problem with animals, are more easily controlled if your dog is confined to its own bed. Getting rid of fleas from a bedroom can be an unnecessary aggravation.

• Some breeds of dog have greasy fur that mars soft furnishings. Animals with dense, short coats are especially likely to cause markings. Therefore, keep them off your bed and, additionally, cover soft furnishings in your living room with old sheets that can be regularly washed and replaced.

## Introducing a new puppy to established pets

He will be apprehensive of his new surroundings, so keep as quiet as you can. Young children are, of course, difficult to restrain but an early explanation to them usually helps. Loud noises will make the puppy run for cover and hide – and be difficult to encourage out.

*Sleep is essential for a puppy's welfare and development into a healthy dog.*

*Carefully introducing a puppy to existing pets results in life-long friendship for them all.*

● Show the puppy his new living area and his eating and drinking bowls. If he starts playing, make these times last no longer than a few minutes, then initiate a rest period.

● Introducing other family pets to him needs care, and while cats may at first keep out of the way and allow themselves time to make an assessment of the 'new boy on the block', dogs are more forward and will make immediate investigations. To begin with, monitor all interactions until you are sure the puppy has been accepted by your other animals as not being a threat.

● Take care that a pup is not overwhelmed and frightened by an established dog. Both need consideration – the puppy to be calmed and welcomed and the dog given greater attention and affection to show that the newcomer will not usurp his status in the home.

● Where possible, take your older and established pet for special walks on his own, when you can spend time lavishing affection and throwing balls for him.

● This settling-in process sometimes takes several weeks, but be calm and patient and ensure your established pets feel secure in your affections.

● Eventually, you may find the puppy and cats snuggling together, or climbing over your dog to get nearer the 'fire!

# PUPPY AND DOG TRAINING

# The importance of training

If puppies are allowed to do just as they wish, they become a misery to themselves as well as their owners. Training a puppy and, later, a dog should be an experience to be enjoyed by both pet and owner and the ensuing companionship of an obedient dog more than repays the effort and time of training. At the end of the training you will both be proud of each other.

## Why is it necessary?

Training will not harm your puppy, but it will enhance his good traits and nature. A few reasons to spend time training him include:

• An untrained puppy seldom becomes fully integrated into a family; he is unaware of a code of behaviour that makes him acceptable to you and to other family pets. He can also be confused about the family (pack) hierarchy.

• He will become a nuisance to neighbours and a danger to pedestrians on footpaths and in recreational areas. He may even chase or bark at cyclists, horses and cars, perhaps causing accidents.

• In rural areas, untrained dogs often revert to their natural instincts and chase sheep and other livestock – a dangerous activity that can result in deaths and a police summons.

• Training puppies not to foul footpaths, recreational areas and places where children play is important, both for the well-being of young people and to avoid a summons and fine.

• It is vital that when fully trained your puppy reacts favourably when he meets other dogs; he should realize that it is not a free-for-all time. He must be kept under control and made to understand that you are 'in charge', even when other dogs are jostling around him.

*An obedient dog is a pleasure to be with – be lavish with praise during his training.*

*Dogs love to run along beaches, but first check that local bye-laws allow this.*

## Training a puppy

This begins early in a pup's life and there are several different stages:

★ Introductory and initial social training as soon as the puppy is brought home (see pages 88–95).

★ Toilet training (see pages 110–111 for details).

★ Obedience training usually starts at the age of six months (see pages 104–107).

## Who's in charge?

Before beginning a puppy's training, an insight into his mind is essential.

★ He is, by nature, a pack animal with an inbred instinct to give allegiance to his pack leader – which is you.

★ Most puppies are highly receptive to training and eager to please, especially if they quickly recognize in you a calm, firm, consistent and reassuring handling nature.

★ Most puppies enjoy the presence of a pack leader, but some breeds are easier to train than others. Those more naturally assertive, such as German Shepherd Dogs and Collies, will require careful and longer training to prevent them attempting to dominate you and the entire household.

## Getting prepared for obedience training

A wide range of collars and chains are available from pet shops and via the internet (see pages 132–133 for details of them as well as their advantages and disadvantages).

Make sure that your puppy is comfortable when wearing a collar or chain or he will be distracted and not respond to you and your commands. Initially, training should be carried out while the puppy is on a lead. Chasing an unleashed puppy around your garden, or across fields and recreational parks, will seem like a game to him, not a time for learning and being obedient.

*Puppies should be made aware that their training is a serious matter, not a time for play and frolics.*

*Puppies must be trained to understand that they must not constantly pull when on a lead.*

## Obedience training sessions

The golden rules when training a puppy are:

★ Initially, only one person (the pack leader) should train the puppy. Later, when training is complete and he knows what is expected of him, another person can take over.

★ Choose a time when the puppy is bright, alert and wide awake. Some puppies have a time when they naturally want to sleep and therefore at that moment are not receptive to being trained.

★ At first, train the puppy for only ten minutes at a time, increasing this as he progresses in his training.

★ Choose a place where the puppy will not be confused or distracted; your garden is an excellent place as he will know it as a friendly environment.

★ Keep your voice pleasant at all times, even when you are exasperated with him. Do not show anger, as this will confuse or frighten him and deter him from cooperating in further training sessions.

★ Remember to praise successes; but do not scold him for failures.

★ There will be days when your puppy is confused and unwilling to be trained; respect this and continue the training the following day.

★ Training is achieved by rewarding success with praise. It is better to ignore misdemeanours than to spoil his determination to please you.

★ Lastly, obedience training should be a happy learning time, for both of you.

# Starting to train your puppy

The day arrives when you and your puppy are about to embark on his training to make him obedient, happy and a close member of your family. Although training sessions can later be undertaken in slight rain, for the first time choose a dry day with little wind to distract him.

> ## The four basic training commands:
>
> ★ 'Sit'   ★ 'Stay'   ★ 'Heel'   ★ 'Come'
>
> These are described and illustrated on pages 104–107.

## Putting on a collar
Very few puppies enjoy having a collar put on them for the first time – it is an unknown element. However, first allowing him to see and sniff at it often alleviates his worries.

In later months and years he will come to realize that the jingling of a collar and chain, especially when combined with the word 'Walkies', heralds an exciting walk.

## Serious learning time
Initially, puppies are not able to understand that the world is not full of 'play'. It is essential to instil into puppies that their training is a serious part of growing up.

At the end of each training session, kneel down, play with him and praise his intelligence.

Follow these basic guidelines:
• Show him the collar and lead to calm his anxieties about wearing them. Put the collar around his neck (check with pages 132–133 that it is correctly positioned).

*A bright, young spaniel obviously eager to take part in a training session.*

• Gently, but firmly, position him on your left side and hold the end of the lead in your right hand. This enables you to calm the puppy with your left hand and to shorten, if necessary, the length of the lead.

• Later, when the puppy is fully trained, you might wish to have the end of the lead only in your left hand with the dog also on your left side. Initially, however, your role is to comfort and control the puppy and this is best accomplished with the puppy on your left side and the end of the lead in your right hand.

• Do not allow him to chew the lead if, by chance, it dangles near his face. Puppies have an inquisitive nature and will chew anything near or at ground level. Therefore, regularly check that obedience training has not turned into a chewing game, rather than an exercise in discipline.

## Left- or right-handed?

Some dog trainers like to have the end of the lead in their left hand, with the puppy or dog on their right side, but normally the other way around is best as it enables a usually stronger arm and hand to be ready to deter and fend off aggressive dogs.

Keeping the dog on your left is essential for gundogs, as most people are right-handed and shoot from the right shoulder. Also, this style of positioning a dog is thought to be a legacy from when war dogs were essentially kept on the left side to enable a right-handed swordsman to swing a sword unhindered.

*Beagles are gregarious and fun-loving dogs and often look at you with an examining gaze.*

# Basic obedience training

Dogs can be trained to a high response level, involving many different and specialized activities. However, for puppies that will develop into family dogs only four basic commands are necessary. Of course, you may later wish to take your dog to dog-training classes and this will involve further training techniques. Initially, however, concentrate on the four major commands – 'Heel', 'Sit', 'Stay' and 'Come'.

## The 'Heel' command

With the collar properly fitted, the lead attached and the puppy confident that you are in complete control of him, give the command 'Heel' and start walking slowly.

● Continue to talk to him in a soft tone to provide the encouragement and confidence that he is doing the right thing and that you are pleased with him. Praise for success always gets a better response than a scold when he has not behaved as required.

● Keep the lead relatively taut to ensure neither you nor the puppy trips over it.

● When you turn, initially always make it to the right so that the puppy has time to react and does not risk having his paws trodden on.

● Do not attempt to make left turns until your puppy is used to walking beside you; otherwise, there is a risk of you falling over him.

● Eventually, the puppy will realize that the proper place for him is close to your left leg.

● When you stop, place your left hand on the puppy's hindquarters and close to his tail; say 'Sit'. He will sit, and this is the next lesson.

● At the end of his first training session, be lavish with praise so that he feels pleased with himself. Keep this first session short – perhaps no more than ten minutes – and ensure he does not become bored or tired.

*With his ears pricked up, this puppy reveals alertness together with a desire to please his handler.*

*Do not allow your puppy to chew the lead when teaching him the "Sit" command.*

## The 'Sit' command

Once your puppy understands the 'Heel' command, he is ready to be taught to sit when requested.

• While walking with the puppy at your side, ask him to sit by using the command 'Sit'. Each time he sits, praise him.

• Ensure he sits at your left side; at the same time as he sits, draw the lead a little tighter (but not choking him). This will ensure there is no risk of him tripping over it or treating a piece of loose lead as something to chew and play with.

• If he tries to lie down, correct him with a small jerk on the lead and, if necessary, lift up his front so that he is sitting, rather than sprawled on the ground.

• Each time you command him to walk and adopt the heel position, slightly loosen the lead to enable him to walk freely and naturally.

• After about a week, and when he has mastered the 'Heel' and 'Sit' commands, try this sequence without attaching him to a lead. If he does this successfully, lavish praise and give a treat. It is a significant point in his training when he understands your commands while not on a lead, and indicates the trust you have in each other.

• These exercises are best undertaken on a daily basis so that he does not forget the routine of walking to heel and then sitting on command.

*Collies are intelligent and keen to show the results of their training. They are superb shepherding dogs.*

## The 'Stay' command

This is a command that is easy for a puppy to understand, especially after mastering the 'Sit' one.

• The 'Stay' command involves training him to sit, with you being able to freely walk around him. Initially, the puppy will still be on a lead, but later should obey this command when free of it.

• Once you are sure he is confident about sitting, remove the lead and slowly move backwards but still looking at him. Ensure there is eye-contact, at the same time holding your right arm up and showing him the open palm of your hand.

• Return to him and praise him.

• If he jumps up to greet you, immediately stop giving him praise and make him go back to the sitting position. Enforce this message by saying 'Stay'. Then repeat the procedure, walking backwards and holding up the palm of your hand. Eventually he will understand and you can lavish praise on him.

• If you carry a few 'treats' in your pocket, he will come to realize that if he does what you ask of him he will be rewarded. Your reward will be the accomplishment of another command.

# The 'Come' command

As soon as your puppy has mastered the 'Stay' command and you are confident that he will remain in position with the lead unattached, you can embark upon the 'Come' command.

• Initially some trainers like to have the puppy on a 'training' lead – a long lead that can be extended and retracted from a handle. However, if you are confident in your puppy's ability to remain in the stay position, it is better not to use it.

• First, put him in the stay position, and make sure he is comfortable and confident before walking away from him, with your back to him. Then turn to face him and call his name, adding 'Come'.

• As soon as he reaches you, immediately give praise and ask him to sit in front of you by saying the command 'Sit'. If he does not sit, do not give praise; instead, repeat the exercise.

• Eventually he will understand what is being asked of him; if he is still being trained on a training lead, now remove it and undertake the 'Come' command without putting a lead on him.

• If you have been undertaking the 'Come' command in your garden, where usually there are few distractions, go through this sequence in a busy area. It is essential that eventually he comes to you on your command, whatever the conditions around him.

*A rapid response is essential on the command 'Come'. Reward such reactions with lavish praise.*

# Puppy fears

When initially young and fresh into this world, most animals are unaware of dangers. They busy around, oblivious of the future and probably keeping close to mum. Young chicks start to recognize fear three or four days after hatching, while for many puppies this happens much later and, usually, quite unexpectedly.

### Fear periods

There is no fixed time when your puppy may become aware of fear. Sometimes, such happenings become apparent during puppy-training classes; animals from herding breeds are more likely to become sensitive to their environment, newly met people and unknown dogs than other breeds. Indeed, German Shepherd Dogs are especially claimed to become apprehensive and fearful – and at an earlier stage than most other breeds.

*Retrievers are usually free from 'fear periods' and therefore well suited to be guide dogs.*

Gundogs may not experience this problem until later – or not at all. For this reason it is no surprise that Labrador Retrievers and their crosses are used as guide dogs, where reliability is essential at all stages in their development. It is also why these dogs are famed as family dogs, where they tolerate the noise and mayhem created by small children.

### Dealing with fear

Whatever the cause of the upset that disquiets and disorientates your puppy, do not shout at him because his reaction is involuntary and solely the result of fear – he cannot help it.

There are occasions when a fear reaction has been accumulating for several weeks, or even months. If this is the case, review your training programme and the way the puppy is treated by your family. Puppies continually need reassurance of their welcome into your home and establishment as a companion animal for the entire family. If just one person ignores them, they may take this to be a sign of non-acceptance, despite an unrestrained welcome give by the rest of the family. This problem can be easily corrected.

At whatever stage of puppyhood your family companion falls prey to fear, here are a few ways to offer help:

● Reassure the puppy that the fear problem is not his fault and that you have unreserved confidence in him. This is a cuddle-and-smiles remedy, together with extra food treats and games.

*Encouraging your puppy or dog to have confidence in his surroundings and people is essential.*

● Identify the problem that initiated fear and avoid such places and circumstances until your pet has re-established confidence in his home life. Then, after four or five days, or longer, and depending on the trauma he experienced, start back on his normal routine.

● Do not confront the puppy with his nemesis. If the problem re-arises while out on a walk, you should immediately turn away and reassure him that it is not his fault. Throwing a ball, for instance, in a park or field can soon take his mind off the problem.

● When you think your pet is over the problem – and there is no way to determine this in advance – ensure he realizes he is loved and wanted. Family walks and games indoors are certain ways for him to regain confidence in himself.

*Unexpected weather, such as snow, may initially cause consternation but usually the animal adapts to it.*

# Toilet training

Teaching toilet manners to a puppy is essential if he is to become a civilized member of a family. When you take over the puppy – ideally at some time between eight and 12 weeks of age – he is unlikely to have received any toilet training; when young, the mother would have 'cleaned up' her puppies. He is therefore now venturing into new territory and needs your guidance.

## Early days

Whether or not you have a garden, it is essential to provide your puppy with a toilet area. Indoors, an old children's play-pen is an ideal way to ensure only a small area is 'at risk' – cover the floor in a sheet of plastic, with several layers of newspaper on top.

*Toilet training a puppy may take several weeks, but is an essential part of his life.*

● Outdoors, create a special area that is out of the way and unlikely to be used by children. Also, ensure the grass is short as anything higher than 5 cm (2 in) will appear to be a jungle and deter your puppy from performing. Puppies like a routine and where possible always encourage the puppy to perform in the same area.

● An added advantage of getting your puppy in spring or early summer, rather than late autumn and winter, is that it is then easier to encourage the pup to go outdoors. It also makes it easy for the puppy's owner to go outside quickly and without having to put on stout and waterproof boots.

● Puppies and dogs are creatures of habit and if fed at the same time each day will also urinate and evacuate their bowels at regular times. Therefore, soon after feeding your puppy encourage him to follow you outside to the allotted area. Using the same phrase when encouraging the pup to go outdoors helps in the routine. The objective is to get the puppy outdoors and with a clear determination to perform. When the deed is done, lavish praise. If the puppy fails to perform, do not offer praise.

● After a time, the puppy will know what is expected of him. Although initially the effort put into toilet training your puppy may appear laborious and repetitious, it avoids having faeces all over your garden; apart from their messiness, dangerous diseases and parasites can be contracted from them.

*Most puppies are quick to learn what is expected of them when being toilet trained.*

# Children and dogs

There can be few sights as pleasing as a dog and child playing together, in a garden, recreational park or at home. They appear to be natural playmates, each full of fun and excitement. Yet care is needed to ensure that a dog is not accidentally and thoughtlessly mistreated. Always check if it is safe to leave a dog on its own with a child. Make sure that the child has been trained as to how to interact with dogs, both the family dog and a dog from outside the home.

*A youngster playing with and talking to a puppy or dog is a near-magical interaction.*

## Safety-first with dogs

Here are a few clues to dog and child safety:

Never...
... tease a puppy or dog as they will not understand the motive and may react angrily.

... disturb a puppy or dog when sleeping – this is an animal's private time and must be respected.

... hold human food and sweets in front of a puppy or dog's face. The animal will become agitated and upset, and will not understand what is happening. He is also likely to snatch at it, so frightening the child. Such food is anyway not suitable for a puppy or dog, especially if based on chocolate.

... allow a child's face to be close to an animal's paws or face.

... encourage a dog to lick a child's face. Should this occur, immediately wash the area with soap and clean water.

... make loud and shrieking noises close to an animal as it may not understand what is happening and therefore react angrily.

... leave a young child alone to play with a dog; an inadvertent pulling of a tail or pushing a finger into the face may result in a sudden and involuntary snap.

## Unfamiliar dogs

Children when in parks often play with their own family's dog, and this is usually safe when monitored by an adult. But the scene quickly changes if an alien dog appears and aggressively bounds up to your dog.

*Never risk being bitten by an aggressive dog as it may result in severe physical injury.*

Should this happen, warn children:
● Never touch the other dog or get between the two animals. The intruding dog may withdraw if your animal adopts a submissive position (usually rolling onto its back). If it turns into a fight, stand well clear.

● Always fend off the animal, rather than fighting back. If you have a bag or coat, try to hold it between the intruding animal and yourself. Unless exceptionally aggressive, the dog will back off after a token barring of teeth and a growl.

● Do not shout or scream at the animal as this may cause a violent reaction. Instead, if possible, indicate to people nearby to call the police.

● Never make eye-contact with a potentially aggressive dog – he will see it as a challenge.

● Talk to the dog in a soft and reassuring tone. Do not run away with your back to the animal.

● Try not to fall over as this will make you more vulnerable to attack. Do not back into a corner either; instead, stand in the open, with plenty of space around you. Try to maintain your mobility.

# Emotional indicators

As with humans, puppies and dogs reveal signs when they are not happy with themselves or people. So be your own animal psychologist and understand their indications of distress.

## Private times

Most puppies and dogs have friendly dispositions, but must not be disturbed during private moments, such as when:

- Eating.

- Sleeping.

- Enjoying a treat such as a chewy or a bone; they are especially protective about these.

- Sick, injured or in pain.

- Excessively tired after a long walk. As age progresses, a dog soon becomes weary after a romp in a park or garden and allowances must be made for this.

- Having, perhaps though old age, vision or hearing problems.

*Whether a puppy or an adult animal, sleep is essential.*

## 'I'm uncomfortable with life' signals

Behavioural signs from puppies and, especially, dogs can point to suffering as well as aggression (see 'Canine anger indicators', page 115). These dog body-language messages – which need swift attention and for the problem to be resolved – include:

- Averting their gaze and looking despondent

- Crouching

- Ears drooping

- Licking lips

- Rolling over onto their back

- Tail tucked under the body

- Tail wagging, but low and slow

- Turning head away and avoiding your look

- Yawning

If you are anxious about your pet's reactions, gain advice from a vet or a dog behaviour specialist. Part of the problem may be through illness, or environment and unsuitable care. Do not leave these problems until they dominate the animal as the sooner they are treated the easier it will be and the better the chance of a full recovery.

*Dogs often play in groups, but sometimes it results in people being attacked.*

## Pack instinct

Dogs are gregarious and, in the wild, hunt, live and play in packs. Therefore, do not be surprised if, when in a group, they become excited and aggressive, especially if they think a 'foreigner' is invading their area or about to inspect their food.

Two or more dogs make a 'pack', which can affect their behaviour. Few people would wish to tangle with a couple of snarling dogs trained as attack animals. But some usually placid animals, if in a group, also can be dangerous when aroused; for that reason unless you are confident of a dog's probity take special care when two dogs are playing near a child.

### Dealing with dog bites

Always treat a dog bite seriously. Immediately visit a local doctor or an accident and emergency unit. Apart from damage to flesh and bones through a severe bite, the relaxation of earlier and well-proven quarantine regulations has increased the risk of a dog having a disease, even maybe rabies.

### Canine anger indicators

Your dog has its own language when displeased or frightened. Anger management is possible – through love, kindness and the routine of family living – but many of the reactions from a dog are natural and just responses to unexpected happenings.

These body-language messages -- which mean you to step away, keep clear and 'respect my space' – include:

★ Barking and snapping

★ Growling noises and baring of teeth

★ Narrowing of eyes

★ Raising of hairs on the animal's neck and back (they may also raise hairs on your neck!)

★ Snarling

# When a new baby arrives

The arrival of a new baby in a family can be confusing for a dog. At one moment he probably considers himself to be the main focus of attention in his pack's life, then suddenly becomes confused by lavish attention being paid to a new arrival. He has probably never experienced anything like this before and therefore feels his status within a family group has been eroded. The situation needs delicate handling if he is to re-harmonize himself within the family and, again, be a happy animal.

*Children and puppies gravitate towards each other, but for success careful preparation is needed.*

## Preparing your dog for the arrival of a new baby

The arrival of a new baby into your family invariably creates major lifestyle changes, and these are certain to affect a dog established in your home.

Dogs are perceptive to even slight changes in a family's routine and long before a new baby arrives your pet will have sensed that 'something is going to happen'. He may become agitated and act quite differently from normal, perhaps being more affectionate to you to further establish his role within your family.

If there is already a baby or small child present in your family, the dog will have a good idea of what to expect. If not, there are a few routine changes you can make to prepare the animal for the arrival of another baby:

● Continue to make a fuss of him – cuddles are a great reassurance to a confused dog.

● Let him see the new pram and cot; at the same time, make a fuss of him and talk about them.

● If possible, in the weeks prior to a baby arriving, play recordings of the noises babies make so that he can get used to them. At the same time as they are playing, talk to him in a reassuring tone (cries, screams and baby chuckles can be confusing when first heard).

● You will need to think about where you are going to sit when looking after your baby; for this reason, position the dog's day-basket out of the way but where he can see you. To him, it must not appear that you are shunting him to a position far away. Make sure that you still have eye-contact with each other.

● Rewarding him with a chew will give your dog reassurance that 'all is well' and that he is still a very important member of the family.

*Dogs are naturally inquisitive about babies, but they need careful introduction to each other.*

### When the baby arrives home

Your dog will be inquisitive about the new arrival and this is quite natural and something to be encouraged.

★ As soon as possible after bringing a new baby into your home, make a fuss of your dog. He will be delighted to see you and also curious about the new arrival.

★ He will be keen to have a look and smell the baby; this needs to be done under strict supervision but in a way that does not alienate him.

★ Dogs which already have babies present in the house will understand the wriggling actions and sounds of babies as being normal, but dogs new to babies might view these actions as those of prey. Therefore, until you are quite certain about the dog, do not leave them together in a room on their own.

# Leaving a dog on its own

Although not recommended, it is inevitable that puppies and dogs are occasionally left on their own for short periods – but preferably for no more than two hours at one time during the day and then only after having become accustomed to it.

Puppies and dogs are gregarious and prefer continuous involvement with their 'pack-family', rather than being left alone. Loneliness makes them feel neglected and from this arises a range of reactions, not triggered through revenge but as a result of insecurity and distress.

*Laces and shoes are toys to a puppy, so put them out of sight in a locked cupboard when you go out.*

## Dire consequences

Each year, many puppies and dogs taken in by animal welfare societies for rehoming are as a result of being left alone for long periods. Owners go off to work and expect the animal to be contented with life; instead, it may bark and cause irritation to neighbours. The problem intensifies and then eventually the animal is taken to an animal welfare society for rehoming. This is not fair on the dog or the welfare society. Therefore, prospective owners who cannot find sufficient time to look after a puppy or dog throughout the life of the animal should not have one.

## Reactions to expect

These are wide-ranging and, no doubt, may enrage you – half-eaten shoes, sugar and jam over the kitchen floor, and gnawed table legs. Whatever your reaction to the mess, never punish or shout at the animal on your return as it will associate this treatment solely with you arriving home, rather than the destruction it created earlier.

A dog's mind is simple when relating cause and effect; it will not remember being naughty and just associate this new and unexpected treatment from you as a further problem.

Symptoms of an animal's distress at being left alone include:

*A puppy or dog left on its own may suffer mental and physical distress.*

• **Visual distress**: This includes trembling and randomly walking or running around the house. Such symptoms may arise as soon as the puppy or dog realizes you are going out and may continue throughout your absence.

• **Vocal distress**: Whining, barking and howling are common, which often causes annoyance to neighbours and further distress to the animal.

• **Aggressive and damaging distress**: This ranges from chewing shoes and ripping clothing to gnawing table legs and carpets.

## Accustoming a puppy or dog to time alone

To ensure a puppy or dog does not become distressed at being left alone, from an early age show that your absence will be short, can be fun and will be accompanied by rewards, such as special praise, toys and treats. This 'absence training' is a gradual process, possibly over four or more weeks; it is progressive, from one stage to another, with each depending on the animal's response to you at each one.

Always be prepared to go back to an earlier stage if the puppy or dog does not respond to you. Should this happen, do not offer praise, but just return the previous stage. Only praise correct responses, not negative ones.

Absence training your puppy or dog:

**1** Initially, ensure your dog is comfortably settled in his basket. Make a fuss of him and give praise as a reward for being obedient. Encourage the animal to stretch out and relax; again with praise.

**2** Move away from the dog and check he remains in the basket. Again, offer praise as a reward. Continue to move away, retaining eye-contact with the animal and giving praise.

**3** Slowly leave the room for a few minutes, then return and give praise if the animal is still in his basket.

**4** Repeat going out of the door for increasingly longer periods, without shutting the door. Then, go out of the front door, again initially for short periods. At each stage, offer praise.

**5** When you are able to go out for ten minutes and the dog is happy and does not show signs of distress, slowly increase this to an hour.

## Keeping him happy when left alone

There are several well-tried ways to keep your dog contented and occupied when on his own. Indeed, because of the expectancy of a treat some dogs even appear to look forward to your departure!

As you prepare to go out, adopt a routine of giving your dog a bone or long, chewy treat that takes some time to 'get at'. This activity takes his mind off you leaving to go out; but such treats must be special and only associated, in the dog's mind, as 'absence treats'.

Ensure that this extra food does not lead to obesity; adjust the amount of other food given to him.

*Ensuring your puppy or dog has a comfortable basket when you are out helps to alleviate loneliness.*

*Giving a dog a treat when you leave home helps to make your absence more acceptable.*

## Sight and sound!

All puppies and dogs, but especially middle-aged and senior-citizen ones, are comforted by sound and pictures when you are away from home. A radio gently playing in the background offers continuity and a strong sense of not being alone, while a digital television has the addition of moving pictures that a dog can easily see. (Incidentally, analogue pictures are transmitted differently and dogs are not able to appreciate them.)

Research suggests that 'soap operas' have most appeal for dogs and these apparently set tails wagging. Sensibly, dogs are not keen on noisy game shows, which are claimed to be a big 'turn-off' for canines.

Dogs are able to associate a show's theme-tune with a programme they like. Therefore, if you intend to leave a programme running on your television while you are away, choose one preferred by your dog. However, continuously watching television programmes may, eventually, lead to your dog being obese – so limit his viewing and take him for regular walks.

### Walkies and toilet trips

Before leaving home, let your dog into your garden to ensure there is an opportunity for him to attend to his toilet needs. Preferably, however, it is better to take the dog for a walk, so that he can not only relieve himself but also work off excess energy before being left alone.

*A fuss and face-to-face chat helps to reassure a dog that you still love him.*

# GROOMING, WALKING AND GENERAL CARE

*Many dogs delight in the extra attention given to them when being groomed.*

Grooming, walking and general care

# Grooming your dog

Grooming a puppy or dog is essential for the animal's welfare – it is also therapeutic for you. It is an excellent way to show your puppy or dog that he is an essential member of your tribe, and provides an opportunity for him to reward you by wagging his tail in appreciation! Also, essentially, it is a good way to detect early signs of parasites such as fleas (see pages 152–153).

## Why groom?

Regularly brushing and combing your puppy or dog removes loose hairs, tangled areas in the coat, dead skin and dust; also, it is a chance to free him of any seedheads his coat may have picked up when passing through grasses and other plants. It also helps to massage the skin and to improve the animal's muscle tone.

## How much should I groom?

The amount of daily brushing and combing needed depends on the coat, that is whether your dog's breed is short-haired, medium-haired, long-haired, wire-haired or woolly (see below and page 126 for the breeds which have coats with these characteristics). Some coats need only a brush, but others require more extensive treatment.

## Establish a routine

Whatever the nature of the coat, getting a puppy used to being groomed at an early stage is essential, as it will become a routine in his life for many years. Try to make the experience fun and enjoyable and he will look forward to it each day.

## Long-haired breeds

Obviously, these are more difficult to keep clean than short-haired types and need regular attention. Also, their coats tend to pick up seedheads and these often become embedded in the coat. Some long-haired breeds have a coat which spills over their eyes and if left causes vision problems.

Breeds include:
- Afghan Hound (see page 38)
- Chow Chow (see page 80)
- Maltese (see page 73)
- Old English Sheepdog (see page 65)
- Pekingese (see page 75)
- Pomeranian (see page 75)
- Rough-coated Collie (see page 64)
- Samoyed (see page 84)
- Shih Tzu (see page 78)
- Yorkshire Terrier (see page 78)

*Grooming a dog encourages a close rapport between the animal and the groomer.*

## Medium-haired breeds

These have coats that are relatively easy to keep clean and free from seedheads.

Breeds include:
- Border Terrier (see page 47)
- Cairn Terrier (see page 49)
- German Shepherd Dog (see page 65)
- Labrador Retriever (see page 61)
- Saluki (see page 44)
- Welsh Corgi (see page 67)

*Although a dog may appear bored when being groomed, be assured that it 'does him good'.*

## Short-haired breeds

These are more easily brushed and kept clean than members of long-haired breeds. However, because their coats are short, in cold areas they may benefit from a dog-coat in winter. As well as keeping an animal warm, it prevents water totally saturating the coat.

Breeds include:
- Basset Hound (see page 39)
- Beagle (see page 39)
- Boxer (see page 79)
- Dobermann Pinscher (see page 81)
- Great Dane (see page 82)
- Greyhound (see page 43)
- Pointer (see page 62)
- Pug (see page 76)
- Smooth-coated Dachshund (see page 41)
- Weimaraner (see page 85)
- Whippet (see page 45)

## Wire-haired breeds

These need grooming with a very stiff brush and a metal comb, preferably every day. Additionally, many terriers benefit from being 'stripped' in summer. This involves clipping the coat and is best undertaken by a professional dog groomer.

Breeds include:
- Airedale Terrier (see page 46)
- Griffon (see page 70)
- Irish Terrier (see page 50)
- Irish Wolfhound (see page 43)
- Schnauzer (see page 85)
- Sealyham Terrier (see page 52)
- West Highland White Terrier (see page 55)
- Wire-haired Fox Terrier (see page 55)

## Woolly-haired breeds

These have woolly-natured coats; they do not moult but often need expert clipping in summer. The coat also requires regular brushing to keep it free from dirt and seedheads.

Breeds include:
- Bedlington Terrier (see page 47)
- Poodle (see pages 83)

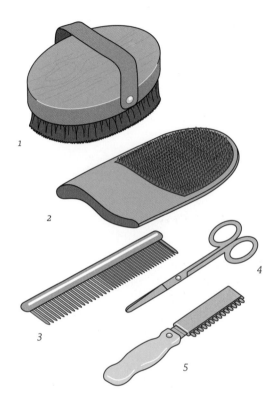

1 Sometimes known as a dandy brush, the looped handle enables you to hold the brush securely, ideal for medium- and long-haired breeds. 2 Mitt for short-haired breeds. One side has short bristles; the other is formed of ribbed fabric. 3 Metal comb for long-haired breeds, especially when a coat is tangled. 4 Scissors for trimming hair between nails to prevent it becoming matted; also useful for cutting hair around the anus to prevent matting as a result of dried faeces. 5 Stripping comb for breeds which are regularly stripped, although this is usually best left to experts. It both combs and cuts.

## Grooming techniques

- **Long-haired breeds**: Use a nylon or natural bristle brush and a metal comb. A curry comb is also useful for removing loose hair while the dog is moulting.

Technique: Brush first (always along the nap of the coat), then comb. Carefully use scissors where the coat is falling over the animal's eyes. A saw-edged stripping comb is often useful to remove loose hairs; this is especially needed in summer when heavy-coated breeds may suffer from high temperatures and overheating.

- **Medium-haired breeds**: Use a nylon or natural bristle brush and a metal comb.

Technique: Brush first (always along the nap of the coat), then comb.

- **Short-haired breeds**: Use a mitt (this is also sometimes known as a hound-glove), which has short wire bristles on one side, and a ribbed fabric on the other. Also use a brush and metal comb.

Technique: First, groom with the bristle side of the mitt, then stroke hard with the fabric side.

- **Wire-haired breeds**: A very stiff brush is needed. A mitt is also useful.

Technique: Take care, especially where the coat is short, not to harm the animal.

- **Woolly-haired breeds**: Use a nylon or natural bristle brush. A metal comb is also useful.

Technique: Mainly rely on the brush, first to remove tangles and then to smooth the coat. Take care, however, not to use it too vigorously.

# Bathing your dog

Water and dogs are a natural combination, but care is essential when you are washing them. Here is some advice on how best to bathe an animal successfully and safely.

*Smooth-coated dogs are easy to wash and shampoo as the suds are soon rinsed off with clean water.*

• Bathing is not usually recommended for puppies under six months of age. However, should your puppy have an accident and become smothered in dirt, use a proprietary puppy or dog shampoo but take care to thoroughly wash it off the coat, using plenty of water but not frightening the puppy. Then towel-dry the coat and finish by using a hairdryer.

*As soon as a dog has been shampooed and thoroughly rinsed, quickly dry with a towel and hairdryer.*

• When introducing a puppy to a hairdryer, make it a 'fun' time; do not use it with an excessively high temperature or for too long as the coat may then become brittle.

• All dogs need to be bathed when dirty or smelly; many delight in paddling through dirty streams, rolling in mud and muck, and wading into the sea. When this happens, bathe them before the dirt dries and becomes caked into their coats.

• Excessively bathing your dog, however, can cause the coat to become dry and brittle, depriving it of natural oils and removing its gloss. Many dog experts suggest no more than two or three baths a year, but if a dog becomes caked in mud and salt water which has dried, a bath is the only way to remove it.

• Use a proprietary dog shampoo, then wash it off several times and towel-dry the coat. Finish off with moderately warm air from a hairdryer. It is usually then necessary to brush and groom the coat.

• When washing extra-large breeds, the best way is to use a hosepipe, but only on a warm day. This usually requires the service of two or three people – preferably wearing swimming costumes or old clothing!

## Drying a dog after a walk

After a walk when the weather is dry, all that is needed is to wipe dirt from the dog's feet. A winter's walk often produces different results, and before leaving home it is wise to be prepared for your return.

Have a couple of old towels ready, and as soon as the dog is indoors start to dry him. If you wait, there is a chance of the animal shaking himself and splattering the floor and cupboards (and you!) with water and dirt.

*Breeds such as the Poodle delight in being washed and made beautiful. Others are rebellious – so take care!*

# Teeth, nails, paws, nose, eyes and ears

It is just as important to keep your dog's teeth, nails, nose, eyes and ears clean as it is to groom its coat. Cleaning also provides an opportunity to check these aspects thoroughly.

## Cleaning a dog's teeth

Puppies, as well as dogs, benefit from having their teeth brushed, and this is best begun at an early age. It helps to prevent the build-up of plaque (sticky or hard material containing bacteria deposited on the surface of teeth) and tartar (a hard substance deposited on teeth by saliva and, in part, consisting of calcium phosphate and mucus).

• Puppy and dog toothbrushes are available, together with 'doggy scrumptious' toothpaste.

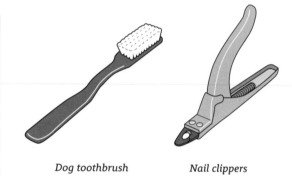

*Dog toothbrush*          *Nail clippers*

• Initially, make tooth cleaning a game, so that the puppy readily cooperates.

• Puppies and dogs most at risk from plaque and tartar are short-faced and toy breeds, which inevitably have mouths packed with overcrowded teeth.

• If deposits accumulate on teeth, it results in receding gums, teeth becoming loosened in the gums, and very bad breath. Should bad breath continue even after several brushings of teeth, consult a vet as it may be caused by another problem.

## Nail clipping

A puppy's claws should not be clipped while the animal is still young. Once it has completed its vaccinations and been allowed outdoors, it will naturally wear down its claws when walking on hard surfaces. If claws are clipped before this stage, there is the possibility of them losing their curved shape and thereby growing straight.

*Most dogs do not protest about having their teeth cleaned, especially if this is followed by a treat.*

*Always use sharp nail clippers that cut cleanly and quickly without causing distress to the animal.*

The nails of dogs may require clipping, although regular walks on pavements usually keeps them short. However, some light-footed breeds, such as the Poodle, may fail to wear down their claws naturally. If this happens, initially consult a vet. When a dog is accustomed to having its nails clipped, it is possible to undertake this task yourself. Use animal nail clippers to carefully trim excessively long nails, but take extreme care not to cut into the base of the nail, where there are nerves and a supply of blood.

## Paws

Inspect these for dirt and hair accumulating between the pads. This can usually be removed by using scissors to cut away excess hair and a moist sponge to remove dirt. If the hair is severely compacted, however, consult a vet.

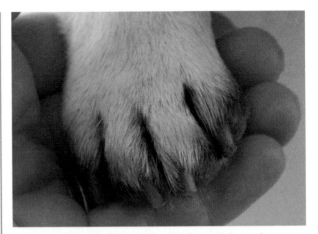

*Never closely cut back the nails – it is better to leave them slightly too long than too short.*

## Nose and eyes

These must be free from discharge; if they are at all cloudy or weeping, consult a vet.

## Ears

Especially check animals with long ears, such as spaniels; they should be free from discharge, dirt and seedheads.

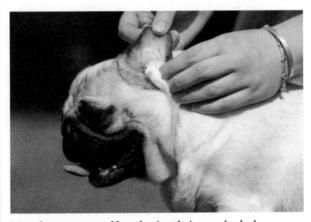

*Most dogs are agreeable to having their ears checked. Throughout the process, reassure the animal by talking to it.*

# Collars, chains and leads

Keeping control of a dog, especially when on a public highway, is vital, and collars, chains and leads help in this task. These must be chosen with care to ensure they fit and do not harm the animal.

*Choose a collar and lead to suit the breed; large and heavy dogs need strong equipment.*

## Collars

When in a public place it is a legal requirement for a dog to wear a collar bearing the owner's name and address. There are several types of collar to be considered:

● **Broad collars**: These are ideal for long-necked breeds. As guidance to its size, it should be possible to slip two fingers between the collar and the dog's neck.

- **Round collars**: Some dogs find these more comfortable, as they move easily up and down the neck.

- **'Halti' head collar**: This slips over the dog's face and is secured by a clip around its neck. A lead is clipped to a ring in the chin area of the 'Halti'; this means that should the dog pull he can be easily corrected.

- **Check chain**: Sometimes known as a 'choke chain', unless put around a dog's neck in the correct manner it can result in the animal choking. It has to be positioned on the neck so that it loosens immediately the dog stops pulling. If used incorrectly it can inflict serious injury on the animal. It is not suitable for long-haired dogs, especially small ones.

Indeed, such is the danger of harming a dog from this style of collar that few people now recommend it.

- **Harnesses**: Ideal for small, miniature and toy dogs.

## Leads

These must be strong and securely attached to the collar. There are two main types:

- **Fixed-length leads**: These usually have a loop-type handle at one end (for you to hold) and a clip-like device at the other for securing to the collar. These leads are 1.2–1.8 m (4–6 ft) long and ensure that both you and the animal know where each other is – at all times.

- **Retractable leads**: Sometimes known as 'training' leads, they have become increasingly popular in recent years; one end clips onto a collar and the other is formed of a handle that enables the lead to be extended to about 5 m (16 ft) long, and then, as required, shortened.

This type of lead has both devotees and critics and its success or failure depends on its use. If used to initially train a dog it does not give total control of the animal and this can cause confusion in the animal's mind. However, if used later, when the animal knows how to behave, it can be of value when used in recreational areas to ensure that the dog does not wander too far.

Its main failure is when used on pavement areas alongside roads; it allows the animal suddenly to race into the road and cause an accident.

*Make sure dogs do not defecate on beaches, especially from early spring to late autumn.*

## Poop-scoops

It is a legal offence to allow a dog to defecate in a public area without removing the mess and disposing of it correctly. Many designs of poop-scoops are available, but essentially they must be easy to use, of a size suitable to the breed of dog, and be able to be carried to a point where the mess can be deposited.

Excrement (faeces) left on playing fields can result in the spread of diseases.

# Exercising your dog

One of the many pleasures in having a dog is going for a walk – whether it is sunny or teeming with rain! Therefore, always ensure you have suitable clothing and footwear that will keep you warm, dry and happy. Your dog will always be excited and ready to take up the challenge of a walk and needs you to play your part, perhaps throwing safely sized balls (which cannot be swallowed) for chasing and retrieving.

## Warning about sticks

For a long time it was thought fun to throw a stick for a dog to catch. However, there have been an increasing number of incidents where the mouths, tongues and throats of dogs have been damaged through this activity and for your pet's sake it is wise to stop throwing sticks.

When a stick is thrown it sometimes becomes embedded in the ground and a dog attempting to pick it up while running at speed can push it further into the ground and there is a great risk of it becoming jammed in its mouth. This causes lacerations to the tongue and throat, as well as damaging the dog's teeth. It may also initiate abscesses in the face or neck.

If a stick does become wedged in your dog's throat, or causes damage to gums and teeth, immediately make contact with a vet.

Throwing toys are available; they are safe to throw, are brightly coloured for easy retrieval, have rounded ends, are textured to maintain a dog's interest and are made from tough, non-toxic rubber. They are available in several sizes to suit your dog.

## Walking next to and across roads

Whatever the distance between your home and the field or recreational park you normally visit with your dog, it often begins on a pavement alongside a road. In these circumstances it is legally essential to have the dog on a lead and to be in control of it.

Always make your dog sit at the kerb area before crossing a road, whether or not vehicles are in sight. It is a matter of routine and at some time may save your pet's life. Use the command 'Sit' when arriving at a kerb, and 'Walk' when it is safe to cross.

## Rules and regulations

Many places where you take your dog have restrictions to protect other people who are using them.

- **Recreational areas**: These include local parks, cricket and football areas. For the safety and health of everyone, these are areas where dogs are banned (especially where children play). There are serious fines for an owner who allows a dog to foul public places.

- **Seaside and beaches**: Dogs frolicking and running through surf are idealistic scenarios and not a problem on beaches where there are few other people, but in summer on crowded beaches they are an ill match and are usually banned through local byelaws.

- **Countryside walks**: Always remain in control and within calling and visual contact of your dog, especially when you know there are sheep, horses and cattle in the vicinity. Should your dog worry livestock, you will be held responsible and possibly face being prosecuted.

In some circumstances, farmers have the right to shoot a dog for worrying livestock.

- **National parks**: These often have their own rules and regulations for the conduct of dogs and responsibilities of owners. Usually, they are not excessively restrictive but essential for the protection of livestock, wild animals and other users of the area. Always check first.

## Your dog's canine friends

It is inevitable that if you take your dog to the same place every day, and at the same time, both of you are going to make friends with other people and dogs. At first, check that he is meeting friendly dogs which will result in extra sport for him. However, should an unknown dog hover in the area, put a lead on your dog until you know more about the new dog's character.

Do not be surprised if, to your dog-walking acquaintances, you initially become known as 'Mrs Sheba' or 'Mr Spot' – it is all part of getting to know like-minded people.

## The amount of exercise required

This is very much influenced by the breed of dog as well as its age.

- Don't force dogs to go for long walks if they are not enjoying the experience. Take special care of puppies of all breeds, also miniature and toy dogs, which soon become tired.

- As a dog ages, it naturally slows down and does not require walks of the length it enjoyed a few years earlier. This especially applies if the animal is suffering from arthritis or other activity-restricting disorder.

- If the animal is physically well, a couple of walks each day are essential.

- When dogs are not give sufficient exercise, they become restless, bored and unhappy; all breeds, especially active ones, such as gun, pastoral and terrier types, are able to tackle 8–13 kilometres (5–8 miles) each day. However, some breeds, such as the Bulldog, do not like sustained walking.

- Walking your dog is equally good for you and provides an excellent reason to get out into the country, either just the two of you or with friends and family.

*Ensure puppies and young dogs are not completely exhausted by a walk as this takes away the fun.*

# FEEDING PUPPIES AND DOGS

# Feeding a puppy

Providing your puppy – and later a dog – with nourishing and tasty food is essential for general good health as well as longevity. Dogs are classified as carnivores and, as such, primarily eat meat. High-quality protein, fats and carbohydrates also need to be included in their diet.

## Vegetarian dogs?

Occasionally, owners who favour a vegetarian diet for themselves consider introducing their puppy or dog to the same regime. This is possible but must be undertaken with care and under the guidance of a vet. Non-meat dog food is available but should never be given to puppies; also, never suddenly change from a meat-based diet to a vegetarian one.

Hundreds of thousands of years of canine evolution have accustomed the stomachs of puppies and dogs to a carnivore diet and they are not suited to a sudden change of diet to a vegetarian type.

## Brand loyalty?

Similarly to their owners, puppies and dogs have their own likes and dislikes about food and it may take several weeks to 'get it right'.

Some branded food is specially prepared for puppies, as well as for dogs in their prime and senior-citizen types. Some dogs prefer gravy-based meals, some jelly-based, and others perhaps something more solid.

*Always ensure each puppy or dog has its own eating bowl, as this prevents squabbles occurring.*

Should the food your puppy or dog is eating cause vomiting or a stomach upset, do not be angry about it since it is out of his control – but you will know the food not to give him in the future.

## Feeding newly born and young puppies

Like all youngsters, puppies need careful feeding and a special diet. When newly born and very young, the dam (mother) will suckle them; this is ideal as the mother's milk contains organisms that help in the puppy's defence against diseases.

● In a puppy's first few weeks of life it will suckle on its mother and receive all its required nourishment. There are

*Puppies gain both food and social comfort from suckling at their mother's breast.*

few substitutes for the mother's milk and puppies should be encouraged to suckle until the flow of milk from the mother declines, often at six or seven weeks, although this varies according to the dam and the size of the litter.

• If the litter is large and the milk flow from the dam reduces, puppies can begin to be weaned as early as three weeks old. Initially, encourage puppies to lick small amounts of cow's milk dabbed on their noses.

• When licking and lapping is mastered, try giving pups small amounts of skimmed milk. At the same time, offer them flakes of white fish or boiled and finely shredded chicken.

• By the age of six weeks a pup may be fully weaned (not reliant any more on its mother's milk, but helpful if it continues) and eating four meals a day. Two of these can be finely shredded meat, the other two consisting of milk and puppy meal, cooked rice, baby cereal or porridge.

• Although fully or partly weaned, the pups should remain with their mother for another two weeks. This will give them greater mental stability later in their lives, as well as warmth and comfort at night.

• At eight weeks old it is possible for puppies to be removed from the mother and taken to other homes.

## Starting a new life

This can be a traumatic change for a puppy; introducing a puppy to its new home and family is discussed on pages 86–95, but here is advice about the food it requires.

★ The dog breeder should provide you with a dietary chart for the pup, and some of the food currently given to it. This helps considerably in settling him into a new environment.

★ When 8–16 weeks old, a puppy requires special food and a feeding routine. The food needs to be easily digestible and popular choices are minced meat, flaked fish, cooked rice and porridge, and milk.

★ There are also specially prepared puppy foods that can be added to his food in increasing amounts.

★ Easily accessible fresh, clean water is essential; ensure the pup can reach over the bowl's rim.

★ During this 8–16-week period the puppy needs four meals each day, preferably at 8am, 12 noon, 4pm and 8pm.

★ At about 16 weeks old, reduce the number of meals to three each day. Then, at about six months old, further reduce the meals to two each day.

## The amount of food a puppy needs

The amount of food a puppy needs each day slowly increases. Initially, the pup will have a small stomach and not be able to eat large 'helpings' of food, but this gradually increases with age and size.

Opposite is a guide to the amount of food you can expect your pup to eat, although it will vary from one pup to another. The breeds are grouped according to their size and weight when adult. For guidance of breeds within each of these groupings, see pages 36–37.

Cow's milk should not be given to cats (instead, lacto-free types are recommended), but dogs are able to drink cow's milk. The amount indicated below is the recommended maximum. Up to the age of six months, milk given to a puppy is considered as a food, rather than a drink. After that age, when milk and cereal meals are discontinued, milk (but not taken directly from a refrigerator, when it is too cold to drink) can be offered separately.

*Where a mother is unable to feed her pups, milk can be given through a baby's bottle.*

## Feeding a puppy (each day)

| Breed (size when adult) | 2–4 months | 4–6 months | 6–9 months |
|---|---|---|---|
| **Miniature and toy** 1–4.5 kg (2–10 lb) | 30–60 g (1–2 oz) | 60–85 g (2–3 oz) | 85–110 g (3–4 oz) |
| **Small–sized breeds** 4.5–13.5 kg (10–30 lb) | 60–110 g (2–4 oz) | 110–170 g (4–6 oz) | 170–225 g (6–8 oz) |
| **Medium–sized breeds** 13.5–23 kg (30–50 lb) | 85–170 g (3–6 oz) | 170–250 g (6–9 oz) | 250–335 g (9–12 oz) |
| **Large–sized breeds** 23–36 kg (50–80 lb) | 110–225 g (4–8 oz) | 225–390 g (8–14 oz) | 390–560 g (14–20 oz) |
| **Giant–sized breeds** 36–84 kg (80–185 lb) | 170–335 g (6–12 oz) | 335–560 g (12–20 oz) | 560+ g (20+ oz) |

Add an equal weight of biscuit meal or other cereal to the meat (when weighed raw).

## Puppy milk ration

Milk is an essential part of a puppy's diet, providing much-needed fats, calcium and minerals. Below is a guide to the maximum amount of milk to offer your puppy each day.

| Breed (size when adult) | 2–4 months | 4–6 months | 6–9 months |
|---|---|---|---|
| **Miniature and toy** 1–4.5 kg (2–10 lb) | 70 ml (1/8 pint) | 110 ml (1/5 pint) | 140 ml (1/4 pint) |
| **Small–sized breeds** 4.5–13.5 kg (10–30 lb) | 140 ml (1/4 pint) | 140 ml (1/4 pint) | 140 ml (1/4 pint) |
| **Medium–sized breeds** 13.5–23 kg (30–50 lb) | 280 ml (1/2 pint) | 280 ml (1/2 pint) | 280 ml (1/2 pint) |
| **Large–sized breeds** 23–36 kg (50–80 lb) | 425 ml (3/4 pint) | 570 ml (1 pint) | 570 ml (1 pint) |
| **Giant–sized breeds** 36–84 kg (80–185 lb) | 570 ml (1 pint) | 855 ml (1 1/2 pints) | 855 ml (1 1/2 pints) |

# Feeding an adult dog

By the age of ten months, your puppy will have grown physically into an adult animal, putting on quite a lot of weight and acquiring muscle. He will probably be full of energy – rushing and bouncing around your house and eager to go on walks; at this stage, he needs a healthy, balanced diet that is formed of high-quality protein, fats and carbohydrates.

Your dog will gain sufficient protein from meals containing fish and meat, and occasionally eggs and cheese. Fats are found in milk and other dairy products, as well as meat and some fish. Carbohydrates are present in biscuits and cereals.

● **Feeding times**: These are a matter of choice and routine. Large-breed dogs have relatively large stomachs and are able to cope with just one meal a day. However, giant-breed dogs, such as the Irish Wolfhound and the Great Dane, require so much food that they cannot take all of their daily ration at one time. They are therefore best given two meals each day.

Small dogs – as well as old dogs – are also best fed twice a day. Medium-sized dogs can also be fed twice a day, with a meal of cereal or biscuit, plus milk, given in the morning and the main meal, usually of meat, in the evening.

Whenever a dog is fed, it must be established as a routine so that the animal knows what to expect – and when. Also, always feed your dog after coming home from a walk, not before. This is especially important during warm weather; the dog can then have a meal and drink of water before retiring for a sleep.

● **Convenience foods**: Sometimes known as 'prepared foods', these offer easy and quickly presented meals for dogs and are ideal where an owner's time for the preparation of fresh dog food is limited.

Some of these foods are 'all-meat' types, which need the addition of cereal or biscuit. However, completely dried-food types suit many dogs and their nutritional requirements, but occasionally need to be supplemented with fresh meat and other foods. Remember that complete dried food will make your dog thirsty and therefore plenty of fresh water must be available to him – throughout the day.

Surprisingly, dogs do not need a regular change in their diets. Therefore, once you have found a food that suits him, do not change it; changing a diet may encourage upset stomachs.

● **Fresh food**: Traditionally, this is the way dogs were fed, especially where families had several animals. This way of feeding dogs is returning to popularity with BARF (Bones And Raw Food) diets. These can be purchased ready to present to your dog.

High-quality fresh meat can be fed raw; alternatively, an economic way is to buy minced beef and inexpensive cuts, such as ox cheek, and mix them with cheap liver and offal. This should be well cooked before offering it to a dog – and needs to be accompanied by biscuit with added vitamins and minerals.

On a warning note, do not feed offal to dogs too often as it may result in diarrhoea.

- **Biscuits and cereal**: These are a main source of carbohydrates in a dog's diet and can be fed on their own or sprinkled on the top of meat at the normal feeding time.

- **Snacks and treats**: Large dog biscuits are excellent between meal treats as they contain minerals and carbohydrates; plus, they are excellent for a dog's teeth.

- **Vegetables**: Although by nature carnivorous, dogs will eat small amounts of cooked vegetables, which can be put into their food for added roughage. These include carrots and cooked potatoes.

- **Bones**: Dogs consider these as special treats, but really they are essential to enable a dog to clean its teeth and massage its gums. To a dog, a bone can become a treasured possession, something to be gnawed at for 'hours and hours' and then hidden for later eating and gnawing. Some dogs will bury and hide them in gardens, while others push them under beds and settees! If you find one it is best to leave it where it is – it demands respect.

Take care not to offer your dog cooked bones that splinter, such as those from lamb, chicken or any chop.

- **Drinking water**: This must be readily available and replenished at least once a day, preferably twice a day in summer. This is vital if the dog is being fed dried food.

- **Milk**: Puppies and dogs needing extra nourishment benefit from cow's milk being made available to them. This especially applies to nursing and pregnant bitches.

## How much food?

Don't give your dog over-large helpings of food at any one time. See page 145 for a dog's daily requirements.

*Eating is a serious matter for a dog and he may resent being disturbed, so leave him in peace until he has finished.*

## Treats

Dogs appear from nowhere when children are eating sweets and biscuits and may just sit in front of them and dribble, but do not be tempted to offer them to a dog. Instead, buy something like a chew – there are many types available and some, such as a raw-hide chew, will be a treat as well as helping to massage your dog's gums, keeping them healthy.

Dog biscuits may appear unappetising to humans, but can be ambrosic to dogs; they are not only nourishing but excellent for your pet's gums and teeth.

Use dog-friendly treats as rewards, not part of a normal diet.

## Food treats to avoid

● Chocolate contains a substance called theobromine which dogs metabolize slowly, enabling it to reach toxic levels in their bodies and causing liver damage; it may even result in fatality. Instead, treat them to sugar-free chocolate drops specifically produced for dogs.

*Small treats are ideal for taking on a walk to reward your dog when he reacts correctly.*

*Your dog will look forward to receiving a treat, especially ones he particularly likes.*

● Sweet biscuits and sugary foods are bad for your dog's teeth, as well as causing weight gain.

● Children's sweets, especially toffees, are particularly bad.

## Food sensitivities and intolerances

In the same way that humans acquire difficulties with food, so too can puppies and dogs. These problem are not common, but when they happen it can be confusing to the owner and distressing to the animal.

Symptoms include:

● Weight gain or loss. Sometimes, an animal may appear to be bloated and this often influences stability when walking.

- Skin and ear problems, such as irritation and colour change.

- Lethargy and an unwillingness to do anything except eat and sleep.

- Diarrhoea or stools being loose and coloured light to mid-brown. They may also be extremely smelly.

- Slime-like jelly expelled with the stools.

- Flatulence.

- Hyperactive and aggressive nature, not usually associated with the animal.

## Identifying and dealing with food intolerances

It is essential to identify the symptoms quickly, so that the cause can be determined. Make a list of all foods your puppy or dog has eaten in the last ten days, then relate them to when they were earlier given and did not cause a problem.

Time spent in carefully tracking down the 'culprit' food is well rewarded – but make sure everyone in the household is honest about treats given to your pet.

Sugar, chocolate, milk, soya and wheat products may be the cause. If you suspect one of these, withhold it from the animal's diet and see what happens. However, should the problem continue, make a visit to a vet.

## Feeding an adult dog – daily requirements

This chart details options for feeding your dog with either meat (weight when raw) or canned food.

| | | |
|---|---|---|
| **Miniature and toy**<br>1–4.5 kg (2–10 lb) | Meat: 85–110 g (3–4 oz) | Can: $^1/_3$ to $^1/_2$ |
| **Small–sized breeds**<br>4.5–13.5 kg (10–30 lb) | Meat: Up to 225 g (8 oz) | Can: $^1/_2$ to 1 |
| **Medium–sized breeds**<br>13.5–23 kg (30–50 lb) | Meat: 335 g (12 oz) | Can: 1 to 1 $^1/_2$ |
| **Large–sized breeds**<br>23–36 kg (50–80 lb) | Meat: 560 g (20 oz) | Can: 1 $^1/_2$ to 2 |
| **Giant–sized breeds**<br>36–84 kg (80–185 lb) | Meat: 560–900 g (20–32 oz) | Can: 2 to 3 |

**Please note:**

★ These are 400 g (14 oz) cans.

★ After giving your dog food from a can, always cover its top to prevent the remaining food becoming dry or contaminated with bacteria. This especially applies in summer, when flies are quickly attracted to an opened and uncovered tin of food.

# DEALING WITH MEDICAL AND OTHER PROBLEMS

# Medical conditions and treatment

At some time during their lives, all puppies and dogs require medical attention, either of a first-aid nature or from a qualified veterinary surgeon (usually just known as a vet). Additionally, puppies need to be vaccinated and booster jabs given to dogs, especially if they are later to be put into boarding kennels.

## Early treatment

Looking after animals and caring for their medical requirements is a responsibility not to be shirked. It is easy to see when an animal is in distress, but can be difficult to diagnose the problem and solution. Therefore, never hesitate to gain advice from a vet.

Many of the common illnesses and disorders which your pet may encounter are described in this chapter, but remember the golden rule when your puppy or dog is unwell – the sooner treatment is given the greater the chance for a full and rapid recovery.

## Abrasions

Those which are slight can be cleaned with a solution of warm water and an antiseptic, then covered with a clean and sterile bandage. Replace the bandage daily, cleaning the wound at every change. Ensure that secondary infection cannot contaminate the abrasion.

## Abscesses

These are inflamed and painful swellings, often accompanied by a rise in temperature. They should not be squeezed.

There are two main ways of treating an abscess to encourage it to burst. The first method is to cover the infected area with hot compresses, and the second is to bathe the abscess in a warm solution of salt water. Use an antiseptic solution to clean the area when it bursts.

If the abscess stubbornly refuses to burst, consult a vet.

## Allergies

These are complaints which affect dogs as well as humans. Puppies and dogs sometimes react unfavourably to things they sniff at or eat – these range from specific foods to detergents and plant pollen. The reaction can also be varied, from vomiting to running eyes and red skin.

The best treatment, of course, is not to allow the animal to have contact with them, but dogs wander and their inborn reaction is to sniff at everything and anything that captures their attention. If the problem arises from specific plants in your garden or chemicals in your house, take care to remove.

## Arthritis

This painful and debilitating problem often affects old dogs and especially those of specific breeds. Labradors, for example, are susceptible to arthritis.

Keeping an animal warm and dry helps to reduce the onset of arthritis, but if the problem intensifies consult a vet.

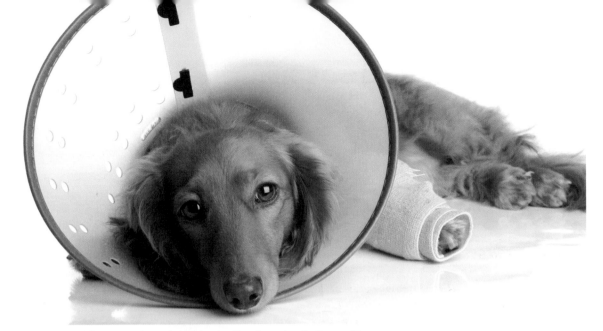

*A 'coned' collar is ideal for preventing a dog biting itself and causing further problems.*

A large, warm basket at night helps to make sleeping easier for the animal. Additionally, there are thermal blankets specially made for arthritic dogs to rest and sleep on.

Anti-inflammatory and pain-killing drugs are available and these usually have to be prescribed and monitored by a vet.

## Bad breath

This is often a sign that the animal is not well; if it lasts for more than three days consult your vet. However, if your dog is young and teething, bad breath is quite normal.

Bad breath often indicates a worm infestation, a stomach infection, tonsillitis, a mouth ulcer, broken teeth, a lip infection or, in elderly dogs, a kidney failure. These are all serious problems.

Apart from seeking medical advice, chlorophyll tablets can be given to the animal, but these cloak the main problem and should not be given immediately prior to visiting a vet as they may confuse a diagnosis.

## Bites

These are usually the result of fights between dogs or with a cat. If they are slight, clean them using an antiseptic solution. However, if the skin has been badly torn, at the earliest opportunity take the animal to see a vet.

Lacerated skin is one of the problems, but more worrying is the chance of the wound being badly infected with harmful bacteria; cats are especially notorious for having teeth that infect an opponent when their bite breaks the skin.

## Bladder infections

This occurs in a wide range of symptoms, including abdominal pain, straining to pass urine, loss of appetite and traces of blood in the urine. All of these conditions will require veterinary treatment.

## Broken teeth

These do not usually hurt a dog, but may cause dribbling or bleeding from the gums. They may also result in bad breath. A consultation with a vet is essential.

## Bronchitis

This causes excessive coughing and is extremely distressing to the animal. Initial home remedies include codeine linctus, but if, after two days, the dog is still suffering, consult a vet.

## Burns and scalds

These usually happen in the home. If the dog is in shock, keep him warm. A drink of warm water and glucose will help but badly burned animals need veterinary help as secondary infection may occur.

## Canker

This is a very painful condition, caused by tiny parasites in the ear. Often, this problem drives a dog to near distraction and may cause fits of hysteria and violent shaking of its head. Take your dog to a vet at the earliest opportunity.

## Canine hepatitis

A highly contagious virus which infects dogs. Symptoms include a fever, depression, loss of appetite, coughing and a tender abdomen. Puppies are inoculated against this virus when eight weeks old, with a further injection later.

*Giving an injection to a puppy or dog is a painless procedure that is usually undertaken by a vet.*

Remember not to allow puppies near other dogs until they have been inoculated.

## Choking

This occurs when the animal's throat is blocked, preventing normal breathing. The animal may be pawing at his mouth, drooling, gagging or coughing. The animal will appear to be in discomfort and, often, whimpering as if in pain. Sometimes, the obstruction clears quickly and on its own, often being coughed up. If not, immediate attention is needed.

Either quickly get your animal to a vet or gain advice over the phone from a veterinary clinic. At this stage, check that the animal is able to breathe – if not, gently pull open the animal's mouth and ensure the tongue is not blocking the throat. If it is, use a finger to hook it forward.

If you can see the blockage, try to release it by using the heel of your hand to give four or five sharp blows between the dog's shoulder blades.

Another way to dislodge the blockage is to hold the animal upside down. For a small or medium-sized dog, hold the animal completely upside down and try to shake out the blockage. However, with a larger animal, you should raise its rear (with the front paws on the ground or a bench) and tilt the head forward.

If you know your dog has only just put something small in his mouth and it appears to have caused a blockage, try the Heimlich Manoeuvre. This involves standing over and behind the animal and encircling his waist. Then, several times, press firmly between the abdomen and ribcage. Do not use excessive force on a small or medium-sized dog as it may be harmed.

## Constipation

This is a problem that occurs from time to time. The puppy or dog can be seen straining to pass a motion; additionally, blood could be coming from the anus and the animal may vomit.

Regular exercise and a balanced diet helps to prevent constipation; proprietary medicines are available to rectify the problem. However, if your dog has not recovered within 24 hours, consult your vet.

## Diarrhoea

Withhold food for a day or so, but ensure the puppy or dog has access to clean, fresh water. This is essential because the animal may become dehydrated and to deprive him of water would cause even more distress.

If the diarrhoea continues for two days in a puppy, or three for a dog, consult your vet.

## Distemper

This is a highly infectious disease and can affect dogs of any age. From contact with a source of infection, the incubation period is 3–15 days before symptoms occur.

Immunity can be provided by vaccination – consult your vet for full details.

Infected puppies and dogs are listless, with a temperature of 40°C (104°F). Animals lose their appetite, develop a dry cough, have a discharge from their eyes and, eventually, suffer from vomiting and diarrhoea. Consult your vet as soon as possible.

## Ear mites

These can cause permanent damage to your puppy's or dog's ears. They are small, eight-legged, spider-like creatures. The problem is first noticed when the puppy or dog repeatedly shakes its head, often losing balance and holding its head at an unusual angle. There may be a discharge from the ear. Consult with a vet at the earliest opportunity.

## Eczema

This is an inflammation of the skin. Often, the dog is irritable, biting and scratching his skin, which becomes red and sore. Hair becomes rubbed way, leaving bare areas. Consult with your vet for treatment.

*Thoroughly checking the inside of a dog's ear requires special medical equipment.*

## Electric shocks

This often happens to puppies and dogs who chew at electric cables. If your puppy or dog is stretched out near a frayed cable it is likely he has received an electrical shock. The first and most important thing to do is to switch off the power.

If an RCD (Residual Current Device) has been fitted into the circuit, the power will have been cut off automatically. However, if it is impossible to judge if power is still passing through the cable, use a broom or piece of wood to pull the cable out of the way.

It is probable that the puppy or dog has urinated, so take care not to stand in it as this may be conducting electricity.

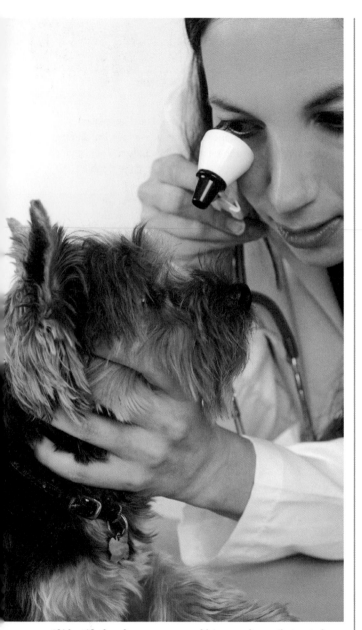

*If identified early, many eye problems can be easily treated with eye drops and lotions.*

## Eye problems

These need professional advice, so consult with a vet as soon as possible.

## Fits

These take several forms and unfortunately there is very little that can be done for the animal other than preventing him from hurting himself or attacking and biting anyone close by. Immediately contact a vet.

## Fleas

These pernicious and widespread pests often plague puppies and dogs, causing irritation and general annoyance. They also transmit the eggs of tapeworms.

Fleas are reddish-brown and crawl through the animal's fur; occasionally, they can be seen jumping through and on top of the fur. They feed by piercing the skin with their mouthparts and sucking blood.

An infestation of fleas also results in the animal's coat becoming covered with flea droppings, the colour of dried blood. There will also be small clots of blood attached to the fur and body; these are the result of skin punctures made by the fleas. These wounds can become infected.

Flea infestations are most likely during warm weather or when central heating is turned on. A flea's life-cycle, from egg to adult, can be as little as 30 days, so unless treatment is given rapidly a small infestation can increase dramatically and became a major debilitating episode in the life of a puppy or dog.

Should an infestation of fleas reach epic proportions, you can expect to have fleas hopping on you, biting your skin and sucking blood.

If you have other dogs, as well as cats, in your home you will need to treat them too – and all at the same time.

Signs and symptoms of flea infestations are:

• Continuous scratching which, if untreated, can send the animal almost demented.
• Fur becomes scratched away, revealing areas of bare skin which, eventually, starts to bleed.
• Black dots of congealed blood show on the animal's fur.
• Brown insects running and jumping on the animal's coat.
• Animals unable to rest and sleep at night through being constantly bitten.
• Animals become irritable, increasingly distressed and miserable.

Flea control involves:

• Spraying or dusting the animal's coat with a recommended insecticide.

• An alternative to spraying or dusting an insecticide is to use a flea control applied directly to the skin on the nape of the animal's neck, between the shoulder blades. This chemical enters the animal's bloodstream, making it toxic to fleas and other blood-sucking creatures.

• Burning or thoroughly washing the animal's bedding.

• Spraying the house, especially the surrounds to the animal's sleeping area, skirting boards, and in corners.

• Using a vacuum cleaner to clean carpets. When complete, remember to throw away or burn the dust bag. Once clean, spray the carpet with a proprietary flea-killing spray.

• Repeat treatment is essential, especially if the initial infestation was severe. Then, throughout the animal's life check for the presence of fleas by parting the fur and looking for their presence.

When treating a puppy, check with your vet to ensure the chemical is suitable.

## Gastritis

This is inflammation of the stomach and usually results from overeating or eating contaminated food. Many breeds of dogs, including Labradors, are notorious scavengers and given the opportunity will raid dustbins.

Symptoms are violent vomiting, accompanied by marked thirst and diarrhoea. Withhold food for a few days, but allow the animal to drink water to prevent dehydration. Then, give the animal light food for two or three days. If the trouble persists, seek advice from a vet.

## Hard pad

This is closely related to distemper, the basic symptoms being the same but with the addition of diarrhoea and the hardening of the foot pads and nose. It is essential to consult a vet as soon as possible.

## Jaundice

This arises when a growth blocks the bile duct, or when a disease prevents the normal secretion of bile. The animal passes orange urine and has a yellowish colouring of the skin. Take the animal to see a vet.

## Leptospirosis

A highly contagious bacterial disease that can be transmitted to humans. It is spread by dogs in their urine; puppies and male animals are more likely to be affected than adult bitches.

Infected animals become lethargic and thirsty, with sore stomachs. This is followed by a high temperature, vomiting and diarrhoea.

A vet must be consulted as soon as possible. Additionally, ensure that all family members wash their hands after touching the animal.

The bacterium attacks the liver and can cause Weil's disease in humans; this is a serious problem that needs urgent medical attention.

*When a dog continually scratches itself it may indicate the presence of fleas or other parasites.*

## Lice

Similarly to fleas, an infestation of lice will make a puppy or dog scratch furiously and repeatedly. There are two types of lice that may infest your animal – one bites and the other sucks. The biting lice cannot pierce the skin; instead, they cluster in large numbers around any body opening, as well as on abrasions. They feed on bodily fluids and other natural secretions. The sucking louse pierces the skin and feeds on blood.

Check for the presence of lice by parting the coat and searching for small, dull and slightly transparent creatures that tend to cling to the animal's skin. Also present will be small, white eggs ('nits') which show up well on dark-coated animals but are difficult to detect on light-coloured breeds.

For puppies, an infestation of lice causes great discomfort and often results in sores from repeatedly scratching; these sometimes become infected. Sucking lice may also cause anaemia, while biting lice transmit tapeworms to your puppy or dog.

The eggs or nits hatch within 7–10 days from being laid and the young mature at about 14 days. Female lice, once fertilized, lay several eggs each day for the remainder of their lives, usually about 30 days. Therefore, once established and if control is neglected, it does not take lice long to create a major problem for your pet. Home treatments are available, but veterinary help is usually required to ensure that the infestation is removed. It is essential that these parasites are controlled early.

## Mange

A skin disease caused by small, eight-legged creatures called mites. There are two types of mange – demodectic and sarcoptic. With both of these, veterinary treatment is essential.

The symptoms of demodectic mange are loss of hair, bald patches and inflamed skin. It is essential to treat the puppy or dog as soon as symptoms are seen as there is a possibility of the animal becoming permanently bald.

Sarcoptic mange causes skin irritation and scabs, and is contagious to humans as well as puppies and dogs. Therefore, early treatment and isolation are vital.

## Pneumonia

A lung infection caused by either a virus or bacteria. It is associated with a high temperature, coughing and general inertia. It is a serious problem, so consult with a vet at the earliest opportunity.

## Rabies

It is estimated that throughout the world more than 70,000 people die each year from rabies, with indications that it is increasing and reaching epidemic proportions in some countries. It is transmitted to humans through bites from infected dogs and other mammals.

Statutory quarantine laws have kept the British Isles free from dog-infected rabies cases for more than a hundred years, although there was a case in 2002 of a rabid bat biting and infecting a man.

If you should be bitten by a dog – whether or not you suspect it of having rabies – immediately see your own doctor or visit an emergency outpatients department. Do not waste time as early treatment is essential.

## Ringworm

This is not caused by a worm, but a highly contagious disease that affects puppies and dogs as well as humans.

It is identified by the round, bare, encrusted areas it produces in the animal's coat. The disease is soon transmitted to humans and therefore you must not touch an infected animal. Urgent veterinary attention is essential.

## Roundworms

See page 156.

## Tapeworms

See page 157.

## Ticks

These are bloodsucking parasites, more often seen in the countryside than in towns and cities. Each tick is about 6 mm ($1/4$ in) long and plagues animals by embedding itself in the flesh, head first. They feed on blood for a few days, gorging and becoming distended.

Do not pull out a tick as you may leave the head embedded in the animal and cause an abscess. Several home cures exist and one is to dab a little ether on a pad and put it on the tick. When the tick withdraws its head, use tweezers to remove it. Another way is to smear the tick with grease for about 30 minutes, cutting off its air supply.

Special tick-removing tools are available but, if you are in doubt about removing ticks, consult a vet.

As a result of a general rise in temperature in a few parts of the British Isles, there has arisen the risk of exotic ticks, some deadly, being introduced by pets which have travelled abroad. If any signs of these are detected, veterinary advice must be sought immediately.

## Vomiting

Several problems cause animals to be sick, including distemper, indigestion, overeating, nervousness, poisoning, parasites, tumours and tonsillitis. Therefore, if your puppy or dog continues to be sick, you must consult a vet at the earliest possible opportunity.

## Worms

These are often a problem during the first nine months of a puppy's life, producing a range of symptoms, including a pot-belly, bad breath and failure to grow properly.

Look out for the following signs:

• Your pet has staring and wide eyes.

• Its coat becomes coarse and harsh.

• Animals drag themselves along, their rears rubbing along the floor.

• They lick their anal regions.

• Small, rice-like grains in faeces indicate that your puppy or dog has tapeworms (see page 157). If this happens, you must consult your vet immediately.

• If your puppy or dog coughs up or defecates whole worms, these are roundworms (see below). Again, consult your vet.

There are two main types of worm: roundworms and tapeworms. The latter has two variants that affect dogs.

• **Roundworms** (*Toxocara canis*). Also known as Dog Roundworms, these are thin, pink-white, curled and coiled. They usually pass out of the animal in vomit or faeces. Their eggs are so small they cannot be readily identified.

In adult animals the roundworm grows from larvae to adult worm inside the body, with eggs and worms being expelled in faeces. Should another dog eat the larvae, infection occurs and the cycle or infection begins again.

Most puppies are born infected by roundworms, and if they are not treated (or 'wormed') the animal becomes sick; it may even lead to death if the infestation is extensive.

*When your puppy defecates, check the faeces to see if they are free from worms (see above).*

However, with the correct treatment such a serious outcome need not happen.

• **Common Tapeworms** (*Dipylidium caninum*). These have long, segmented strips; regularly, segments break off and are cast out through the host's anus.

These segments contains egg sacs that resemble grains of rice and are often seen around an infected dog's anus. Occasionally, an animal may vomit an entire tapeworm, but this is a rare occurrence.

Dogs are not born with a tapeworm infestation, but can pick it up from other dogs. Additionally, fleas are part of the tapeworm's life-cycle.

Tapeworms develop inside fleas and during a flea infestation and while grooming itself a dog may eat them. Then, an adult tapeworm attaches itself to the dog's intestinal wall. At that stage, the tapeworm can be up to 60 cm (2 ft) long. Gradually, segments break away and are passed out in faeces. Segments break open to release eggs which are, in turn, eaten by fleas. So the cycle continues.

• **Hydatid Worms** or **Hyper Tapeworms** (*Echinococcus granulosus*). This is a more pernicious tapeworm, but it is not so widespread as the Common Tapeworm. It is found in some rural areas of Wales and usually in sheepdogs which have eaten the flesh of infected sheep.

Its life-cycle is complex and includes dogs (and other carnivores) as well as herbivores such as sheep and goats. The best way to prevent dogs being contaminated is to stop them eating offal from infected animals. If this tapeworm becomes present in humans it initiates Hydatid Disease, which causes liver damage. You will see the presence of worms in faeces.

The best way to prevent human infection is through personal hygiene, especially before preparing food and after dealing with dogs and other animals.

## Keeping children – and you – safe

The Roundworm (*Toxocara canis*) is found worldwide and care is essential to prevent humans becoming infected, especially children. Sometimes, an infection can cause retinal damage and blindness.

**Preventing infection includes:**

★ Ensuring that play areas for children cannot be accessed by dogs.

★ Using a poop-scoop to clear up faeces, both in your own garden and when the dog defecates while being taken for a walk.

★ Worming your puppy when young, and adult animals regularly.

★ Clearing away all puppy and dog faeces from your garden. Fresh faeces are not as dangerous as aged ones because roundworm eggs take about three weeks to become infectious (often longer during winter). The eggs remain infectious for up to two years.

★ Puppy worming, which is essential to keep your family healthy and uncontaminated from roundworms. A puppy with roundworms can begin passing roundworm eggs in its faeces when only two to three weeks old.

★ Discouraging children from handling puppies before they have been wormed.

★ Washing hands thoroughly after handling a puppy.

★ Not allowing puppies to lick children's faces.

## Travel sickness

When travelling in a car, many puppies are initially affected by motion sickness. This causes symptoms of panting, nausea and vomiting. Additionally, the anxiety of being in a totally alien environment – and one which is rolling and causing him to become unsettled – may bring about diarrhoea.

Your vet will be able to recommend tranquillizing and anti-motion drugs during the early weeks of car travel but, if care and a good introduction are provided, usually the puppy soon gains enthusiasm for the 'open road'.

*Regularly check on your dog when it is in a car to make sure it is not becoming hot.*

*Take a bowl and a few bottles of drinking water with you when on a car trip with your dog.*

## Heat exhaustion

Puppies and dogs subjected to high temperatures in cars, canvas tents, caravans and cabin cruisers are at serious risk from heat exhaustion.

When in your garden during hot summer days, puppies and dogs can be lightly sprinkled with water, but do not plunge them in a cold bath or swimming pool as it may be too much of a shock to their systems.

# Socializing 'problem' dogs

Encouraging your puppy or dog to be a family member is essential as, like humans, they are gregarious and at their best when part of a group. Most puppies and dogs delight in family attention and soon make it clear they are here to stay. A few, however, appear to withdraw into themselves and shun the world around them.

There are several possible reasons why they adopt this attitude, which is often influenced by their backgrounds, such as:

• Rescued puppies and dogs which have been badly treated by previous owners need extra kindness and encouragement to enable them to settle down and to become part of family life. Those that earlier were physically abused may shy away if they perceive a walking stick – perhaps earlier associated with beatings – being taken out of a rack.

• Puppies and dogs earlier bullied by siblings will also be reticent at integrating with your family and other pets. It takes love, patience and time to show them their value as family members – but it can be done.

• Some puppies and dogs appear to have lost the ability to cope with the pressures of day-to-day life. Why this occurs may not always be clear, but can reveal itself as:
- hiding under chairs when visitors arrive;
- crawling, belly tightly on the floor;
- involuntarily urinating.

• Re-establishing an animal's life is a matter of love, understanding and patience. Here are a few tips for success:
- Do not shout at the animal, even when it makes a mistake. Rather, make an extra fuss when it succeeds.
- If possible, identify the problem that causes it distress. This may be sounds it heard earlier or even a coat similar to one worn by a person who mistreated it. These all initiate flash-

*A young family and dog getting to know each other soon captures attention and elicits smiles.*

backs to when it was frightened or hurt. Open spaces frighten some dogs; they might have been attacked by another dog when in a park or field. Fireworks and the sudden appearance of an aircraft or hot-air balloon can leave dogs traumatized.

Some problems are easily identified and corrected, while others take weeks or months of dedicated attention from you and your entire family. It is essential that the puppy or dog regains confidence in itself and this is best achieved through love and patience, together with a determined effort to understand the cause of the problem.

# Veterinary services

Throughout its life your puppy – then dog – will require specialist advice from a vet. From early injections to information about fleas, lice and worms, the advice offered by a vet is invaluable in resolving problems. At the end of an animal's life, too, an empathic vet is essential for putting your treasured pet to sleep. It is important that you find a vet both you and your puppy or dog feel completely comfortable with.

## Finding a good vet

Whether you have a puppy, a rescued animal from an animal sanctuary or an aged dog you have taken over from a friend or family member, it is essential to find a vet you can trust.

If the animal is from an animal sanctuary, they may be able to recommend a veterinary establishment in your area. Alternatively, ask those of your friends who own dogs for their recommendations.

On your first visit to the veterinary establishment you have selected, check that both the receptionist and vet have empathy with you and your animal. A friendly and interested attitude will go far to reassure you and your pet. Also, note the ambience and cleanliness of the surgery.

Remember that your puppy or dog will be on unfamiliar territory and may show signs of anxiety; he will need plenty of comforting.

## Vaccinations

These are generally essential for the health and long-term well-being of puppies and dogs. They give protection against infectious diseases such as canine hepatitis, canine parvovirus, distemper, kennel cough and leptospirosis. These injections are essential for your animal's good health. Additionally, if you wish to put your dog in kennels, proof will

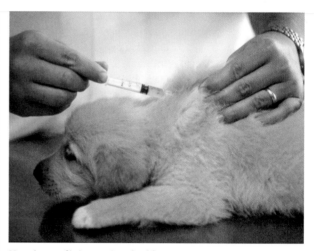

*Veterinary clinics are invaluable repositories of information about the welfare of animals.*

be needed to show that the animal's vaccinations are up to date, or the kennel may refuse to take the dog in.

● Puppies need to be treated twice (consult with your vet to ensure your puppy has the correct vaccination regime).

● Adult dogs may need regular booster vaccinations, at intervals of one or two years. These are very important and should be discussed with your vet.

# A time to go

It is inevitable that towards the end of your treasured pet's life it is necessary to make the difficult decision about ending his existence. There is no firm guide as to when a dog is best put to sleep, but usually it is done when the animal is enfeebled through old age or as a result of an illness.

It is not a problem to know when your pet is in distress, but sometimes difficult to admit it to oneself. It is a human desire to hope for a pet's recovery, even when not feasible. At this stage, take advice from a vet who, from many years of experience at tending to animals, will be able to guide you to the best decision. He will be able to tell you if the animal is in pain and if the problem is incurable. If the answer is that for the dog's own well-being he would be best put to sleep, take the advice.

It is far better to save the animal from unnecessary suffering, and for you to remember him as he was when healthy and in his prime, than to keep a sick and old animal alive. It is a difficult and traumatic decision to put an animal to sleep, and a time for much personal courage.

When the time arrives, do not be embarrassed at showing a vet how upset you are – he or she will understand. Neither should you rush into getting another puppy or dog to replace your treasured friend – give yourself plenty of time to grieve and remember the earlier and golden years with him.

## An alternative direction

When a family loses a treasured dog, they may find the emptiness of the house unbearable. To alleviate this, they could help at an animal sanctuary, or foster a pet.

*Old age enfeebles all dogs and there comes a time when an animal is best put to sleep.*

*Puppies and dogs are usually healthy and active – but sometimes problems occur.*

Dealing with medical and other problems

# First aid

You are likely to be first on the scene when a medical problem affects your puppy or dog in your home, garden or when out for a walk, but always be aware of the limits of your knowledge, and seek professional help urgently if the problem is beyond your ability. If necessary, contact a vet by telephone, giving precise details of the problem and gaining immediate guidance.

An injured puppy or dog will be frightened and disorientated, so keep the animal quiet and warm (but not hot). Talking quietly and reassuringly to the animal before professional help arrives helps to keep the animal calm.

• **Moving an injured puppy**: An injured puppy is best moved by slipping both hands underneath and lifting him to a place of safety. Try not to move his legs. However, if a fracture is suspected, position him with the damaged limb uppermost.

• **Moving an injured dog**: If the animal has been in a road accident, where possible leave him alone but keep him warm. If it is necessary to move the animal, carefully slide a smooth and flat board (slightly larger than the dog when stretched out) underneath.

If the animal is restless, it may be necessary to use wide, soft tape to secure him to the board, but take care not to restrict his breathing.

Where a fracture is not suspected, the animal can be carried to a place of safety.

Sometimes when in a road accident, the animal becomes disorientated and wanders off. Try to prevent this by putting a lead on the animal and settling him in a quiet position until help arrives.

**Cleaning wounds**: While awaiting the arrival of a vet, major bleeding needs to be stopped or stemmed. Place a folded clean handkerchief over the wound and secure it in place with a wide, soft bandage. If necessary, hold the dressing in place until veterinary help arrives.

For lesser wounds, where there is little bleeding, bathe the area in a saline solution of 1 teaspoon of salt to 0.5 litre (1 pint) of slightly warm, clean water. Do not use commercially available antiseptics or disinfectants.

• **Shock**: Apart from an animal being in shock after an accident, this condition may also occur through electrocution (see pages 151 and 169).

Additionally, puppies and dogs can be put into shock through wasp or bee stings. Keep the animal warm and, if necessary, gently massage the chest. Seek medical help urgently.

Shock can result from a wide range of other injuries. Keep the animal warm and, if unconscious, move it onto its side and clear the airways. This involves opening its mouth and ensuring the tongue is to the front of the mouth.

Do not underestimate both the initial and long-term effects of shock. Even after treatment and initial recovery you will need to monitor that the animal is returning to his former good health. If in doubt, consult a vet.

## Administering medicine

If you have never administered medicines to puppies or dogs, it may appear a formidable task. Some animals are cooperative, others need gentle persuasion, while for some the task demands subterfuge on your part.

● **Taking tablets**: Many puppies and dogs will enthusiastically lick a tablet from your hand, especially if they know a 'treat' is waiting for them afterwards. Other animals respond to having the top jaw gently opened with one hand and the lower one kept open with two fingers and a tablet popped on top of the tongue using a thumb and forefinger. Then, close the jaws and gently stroke the throat area downwards. You will be able to feel the animal swallow.

A few animals need the process of taking tablets turned into a game. One method is to cut a few pieces of cheese into small cubes and insert a tablet into one of them. Then, by first giving just pieces of cheese, the animal's appetite is stimulated, enabling the tablet-and-cheese combination to be quickly swallowed.

There are also devices your vet can supply that enable a tablet to be placed at the back of the animal's throat.

If giving an animal a tablet is difficult in any way, ask for guidance from a vet.

● **Liquid medicine**: Some puppies and dogs will lick medicine directly off a spoon. For others, gently easing open the mouth and tipping in the medicine is an alternative.

A further method is, with the aid of a helper, to hold the animal's mouth closed and slightly raised and ease the liquid into a pouch of loose skin at the side of the mouth. When the mouth is released, the animal will swallow and lick the medicine at the side of its mouth.

● **Eye drops**: Usually a helper is needed, both to hold the dog and give it reassurance through kind words. Raise the dog's

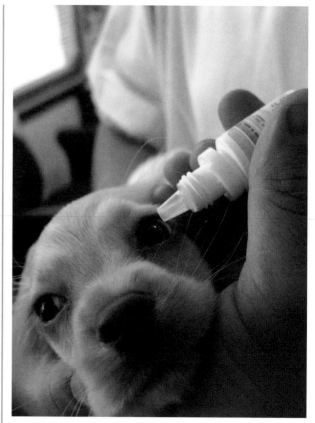

*A carefully positioned 'dropper' enables eye drops to be administered to an animal.*

head slightly and apply drops to the inner corner of the eye. They will then run over the animal's eyeball.

If the animal is taking a course of eye drops, reward him with a treat after each application.

● **Ear drops**: A helper is often needed to reassure the animal that all is well. Hold the animal's head slightly towards one side and apply the drops through a dropper so they run into the ear canal. Afterwards, wipe away excess drops and give the animal a treat.

# Neutering

An unneutered bitch comes into season (a time when she is fertile and likely to conceive and produce puppies) once or twice a year. She remains in this fertile condition for about three weeks, attracting unneutered males. During this period, bitches become over-excited and dogs aggressive. Males use urine to mark their territory and become aggressive and bad-tempered.

- Unneutered males are at risk of testicular cancer as they age.

- Unneutered males will pester females, whether or not they are in season, and this often results in owners becoming angry and vociferous towards you.

- Unneutered females are at risk from pyometra, an infection of the womb, as they get older. Additionally, they may develop mammary tumours.

- An unneutered female when in season may have to be kept indoors to prevent dogs mating with her. This reduces the opportunity to go for walks.

- Neutering is an option to be considered if you do not intend to breed with your dog or bitch and raise puppies. Essentially, before breeding puppies consider what to do with the litter. It is essential to remember that there are a great number of unwanted dogs in the British Isles, as well as the rest of the world. For this reason, animal rescue organizations insist that an adopted animal is neutered.

- Neutering is a simple operation, performed under a general anaesthetic. Females are 'spayed' and this involves the removal of the animal's womb and ovaries. In male animals, the testicles are removed.

Consult a vet about the best age to neuter an animal.

*Animal welfare organizations rightfully stress the advantages of bitches not having unwanted pregnancies.*

# HOUSEHOLD AND GARDEN DANGERS

# Providing a safe environment

Puppies, like all young animals, are inquisitive and without any thought of danger. They totter, bounce and jump around, full of fun and with a strong desire to please and amuse you. However, homes, garages and gardens can be like minefields for them – disasters waiting to happen. Here are some of these dangers and ways to make life safer for your puppy.

*Ensure puppies cannot escape from your garden by squeezing under a fence or gate.*

## Fences, hedges and gates

Puppy-proofing gardens is a formidable task, especially if the garden is large and the puppy hell-bent on escape. Young terriers are often especially determined to tunnel their way out of a garden.

• **Fences**: These have varied constructions and some are easier to puppy-proof than others.
- Close-boarded fences usually have gravel boards along their bases, sealing gaps between its base and the ground.
- Panel fencing invariably is constructed to leave a gap between its base and the ground. This needs to be filled with wire-netting, preferably partly buried in the ground.
- Chestnut paling has gaps at its base; wire-netting is the best gap filler as it can be removed when the puppy grows and cannot fit under it.
- Chain-link fencing results in a gap as its base and the best solution is to fit a gravel board (similar to that at the base of a close-boarded fence).
- Ranch-style fencing and picket fencing invariably have a clear base. These types of fencing have plenty of eye-appeal and therefore do not cloak them with wire-netting for longer than necessary.

• **Gates**: The usual puppy escape route is underneath the gate's base. Wire-netting, temporarily secured to the gate, is usually the only solution.

- **Hedges**: These are more difficult to puppy-proof than any other type of boundary and usually result in trying to manipulate and secure wire-netting along its base. Strong bamboo canes interwoven in the netting help to keep it rigid.

## Garden ponds

Water and puppies are not compatible, whatever the puppy thinks about it! Adult water-loving breeds gravitate towards ponds and streams, but puppies are likely to have accidents as often they are unable to get out. Therefore, securely fence off ponds, streams and waterfalls while your puppy is young.

## Garden tools

Many garden tools have sharp edges and, if left spread in a garden when not in use, can be lethal to puppies. Also, when using lawnmowers, hedgetrimmers, strimmers and similar mechanical tools your immediate attention will not always be on your puppy's safety. Therefore, keep your puppy indoors when using potentially dangerous gardening equipment.

## Electricity and shocks

Electric cables, especially when in use and continually moving, are irresistible to puppies, who invariable snap at them. Fitting a 30 mA RCD (Residual Current Device) in the electrical circuit could help save your puppy's life if the cable is chewed. This device instantly disconnects the supply of electricity when it detects an imbalance between input and output currents.

Remember that puppies and dogs, like all animals, are highly sensitive to electric shocks, and therefore you must always ensure that electricity and puppies are kept apart. Your puppy is especially vulnerable when in a garden as he could be standing on damp ground and thereby likely to form an instant 'earthing' circuit. Remember that once the plug of an appliance has been put into a socket and the current has been turned on, your puppy could be at risk, whether or not the piece of equipment is actually operating.

If your puppy or dog receives an electric shock, he will probably collapse and urinate. If electrical power is still passing through the cable and close to the animal, do not use your hands to attend to the dog. Instead, use a dry, wooden stick or long-handled broom to push the cable away from the dog. First aid can then be given (see page 163).

*Puppies and dogs have a natural instinct to bite and chew, thereby often damaging their gums and teeth.*

*Burrowing under a garden shed is a fun, but dangerous, pastime for puppies and dogs.*

Household and garden dangers

## Garden sheds

Often considered to be oases of contentment and a retreat from the world, to a puppy they are full of captivating smells and, perhaps, an old sack to lie on. But life is not that simple and garden chemicals, household paints and precariously positioned tools can be accidents waiting to happen. Therefore, keep your shed door closed and locked.

## Garages and drives

These are full of dangers. Always make sure you know where your puppy is before starting up your car and driving away. Additionally, before shutting garage doors, check that your puppy is not inside the garage.

Later, when you are trying to get your puppy used to car travel (see pages 174–175), it is likely that the sound of an engine being turned on will encourage your puppy to appear as if from nowhere, full of tail wags and 'smiles'. Therefore, you should always first check on the puppy's whereabouts before starting a car and driving away.

## Log storage

If you store logs outdoors, make certain that your puppy cannot dislodge them and cause a 'log-roll' that lands on top of him and causes injury.

## Decking

The undersides of decking are, to a puppy, areas well worth investigation. Retrieving a trapped puppy from under decking 60 cm (2 ft) high is relatively easy, but where decking is secured to timber bearers, 7.5–10 cm (3–4 in) thick and laid directly on the ground, dismantling parts of it may be the only solution to the retrieval of a puppy. Therefore, block up the ends to prevent the puppy's entry.

## Kitchens

Puppies are often fed in kitchens and some are fortunate to have a basket nestling in a warm, draught-free corner. But ensure these eating, drinking and sleeping places are not positioned where hot water can splash on them.

## Open fires and log-burning stoves

Eventually, puppies learn that the best place – apart from a soft sofa – is near a source of heat, but, like young children, they are inquisitive and may get too near an open flame or a hot stove. While your puppy is growing up, secure a protective fire screen around the fire.

*Eventually, a puppy or dog can be given a shoe of its own to chew – but safeguard all others!*

### Chewing shoes and slippers

Always keep bedroom doors and cupboards closed as puppies love to chew shoes – but usually only one of each pair! And their timing is remarkable – usually just before you are going out for an anniversary evening meal or about to make your way to a wedding.

Giving a puppy an aged, well-worn slipper, steeped in rich smells, is a solution to this problem.

# TRAVELLING AND BOARDING

# Travelling in a car

Puppies generally take to car travel with the same enthusiasm as fish to water. It is a new adventure for them, often part of a family journey and with the opportunity to explore new sights and smells. But they need to be controlled within a car as otherwise their antics could cause accidents.

## Preparing a puppy for car travel

Although puppies eventually enjoy riding in cars, at first they may be sick. Here are a few clues to introducing your puppy to the world of motoring.

• Initially, encourage him to sit in your parked car; when he relaxes give lots or praise and, if he wishes, let him get out or, possibly, leave him there to have a nap.

• Then, take your puppy for a series of short journeys, perhaps about five minutes. You can then judge if he is still enthusiastic for a 'life on the open road'.

• For subsequent journeys, increase the time spent in the car.

• If, after several car journeys, he is still sick, consult your vet for advice. Sedatives or an anti-motion sickness drug may help. Eventually, however, most dogs will become used to car travel.

• It is as well to take a blanket for him to sit on, both to make his journey comfortable and in case he is sick.

• Remember to stop frequently for him to stretch his legs and relieve himself, as well as to have a drink of water.

• Fresh air – but not draughts – is essential, especially throughout summer. Dogs quickly suffer from overheating and this is especially happens in badly ventilated cars.

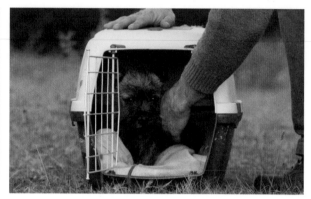

*Keep a puppy or dog secure in a car.*
*Page 172: Never allow a dog to lean out of a window.*

However, regardless of ventilation, you must *never* leave a dog alone in a parked car.

• Take several bottles of clean, fresh water with you, together with a drinking bowl.

• When in a car, remove the dog's lead, but have it ready for when you stop and he needs to be taken for a walk. However, a travelling harness will prevent him from roaming around when in the car (see page 175).

## Legal obligations

Should your dog suffer – or even die – through being locked in a car with all its windows closed, you will be held responsible.

During summer, it takes a locked car only a few minutes for the temperature to rise and a dog to start to suffer. The temperature continues to rise to a point that will 'cook' your dog and bring about a hideous and painful death.

Dogs suffering intense heat often move down into the foot-well part of a car to avoid high temperatures. If, during this period, police have their attention drawn to the suffering of a dog, they are legally enabled to break a window to allow the animal to be removed. Additionally, the owner of the car can expect to be prosecuted.

Every year, dogs die in this way, some even when in the care of professional dog handlers – much to their shame.

### Motoring enthusiasts!

Some breeds have a particular enthusiasm for travelling in cars, almost to the point of mania. These include:

| | |
|---|---|
| ★ Collie | ★ Corgi |
| ★ Great Dane | ★ Italian Greyhound |
| ★ Labrador Retriever | ★ Springer Spaniel |

In addition to these popular breeds, many cross-breeds and mongrels have a passion for motoring.

## Establishing a puppy's travelling position

Unless a puppy's travelling position is made known to him from an early stage, there will be very little chance of later (when he is large and dominant) getting him to travel in a restricted area at the back of a car. Always start his car travel discipline from the onset.

*It is dangerous to drive with an unsecured dog, as well as one that is leaning out of a window.*

Dogs often like sitting with children on the back seat, but the safest place is behind a metal screen that separates the rear of the back seats from the tail-gate.

If the car does not have an open-topped luggage area at its rear (or the space is small), travelling on the back seat is inevitable. Place a piece of plastic over the seat, with a dog blanket on top, and secure the dog with a travelling harness attached to a seat belt. A dog that is secured in this way will not be an added problem during the journey or in the event of an accident.

## Ramped entry

With age, a dog may become unable to jump into the back of a car. At this stage, a wide and secure ramp is essential. This is securely placed on the back of a car, with the other end firmly on the ground. Initially, you may have to encourage your dog to walk up the ramp.

# Boarding kennels

Reliable, clean and secure kennels are essential for your puppy or dog. Kennels are licensed by local authorities and their rules and regulations often differ from one region to another. Nevertheless, when discussing the boarding of your puppy or dog with a kennel, check they are legally entitled to offer boarding facilities to animals. Make sure, too, that they realize they will be looking after your treasured pet.

### Selecting a boarding kennel

Ask your vet to recommend a good and reliable boarding kennel in your area. A veterinary clinic that has been established for five or more years will have received useful feedback from clients about local kennels. Alternatively, other dog owners are a source of information.

### Checking out the establishment

Before officially arranging for a boarding kennel to look after your puppy or dog, visit and inspect it. You will be entrusting your treasured family companion to people you may not know and for both your and your pet's sake a thorough inspection is essential.

• Check that the people who will be in charge of your animal have the necessary professional qualifications. The kennel's local authority licence to operate must be on display – or available on request. You should also ask for confirmation that a vet is on call 24 hours every day. If your pet becomes ill, immediate veterinary assessment and treatment are essential.

• If the establishment looks busy, with happy, smiling people collecting their pets, it is a good sign.

• The attitude of staff should be responsive to your questions, with smiles and vitality.

*Your puppy or dog will miss you – but a good kennel will ensure he is taken for several walks each day.*

• The number of staff must be high to enable your dog to be individually exercised two or three times each day. Alternatively, your dog may be offered a communal run for exercise, but this exposes him to the possibility of cross-infection from other animals.

• Check that the accommodation is clean; it must not have lingering smells and faeces that have not been removed. Feeding dishes must be clean and water bowls filled with fresh water.

• The kitchen where the animals' food is prepared must be clean and well organized to ensure each resident is given the required type and amount of food.

## When booking in your puppy or dog

No reputable boarding kennel will accept your animal unless his vaccinations are up to date. Apart from confirmation of dates, the kennel will need to know:

• Your animal's health record and any particular habits and dietary requirements.

*Some kennels have a repressive nature. Therefore, carefully assess the kennel before leaving your pet in its care.*

• The name and contact details of the vet who normally treats your pet.

• Emergency telephone numbers should veterinary treatment become necessary.

---

### Security

Ensuring your puppy or dog remains safe and confined within the establishment is essential. Check that doors can be securely locked, without risk of animals escaping. A door needs only to be open for a few seconds for a dog to escape.

---

*Always ensure your puppy or dog has been vaccinated before putting him in a kennel.*

# DOGS AND THE LAW

# Legal considerations

Having a puppy or dog as a family pet or personal companion is one of the greatest pleasures of life and one steeped in love and empathy. However, it is a collaboration between dog and owner that must be within the framework of the law, for both the animal's well-being and that of the community. Some of these requirements are common sense; others are enforced within a legal framework.

## Dog registration

Within the British Isles, the traditional dog licence was abolished in 1988, but since then major animal welfare organizations have campaigned for all dogs to be micro-chipped. This is the implanting of a silicone chip within a dog's body that enables it to be identified through the use of a scanner.

Microchipping is painless to the animal and no more complicated than a normal injection. It can be undertaken by a vet or properly qualified person; there is a charge for this service, but it is well worth the cost.

Many vets, dog wardens and major animal welfare societies have scanners able to read the chip and identify the owner and address. This enables escaped puppies and dogs to be identified and quickly reunited with their owners. However, there is one major problem with this identification process, in that a single scanner does not read all microchips. This technical difficulty is being addressed, but meanwhile if your pet is lost it is advisable to try all avenues of enquiry, including those detailed below.

## Stray dogs

This is a major problem within many communities, causing road accidents as well as fouling footpaths and verges alongside roads. Vagrant dogs may also attack people and other animals.

Dog wardens are legally obliged to catch, remove and detain offending animals. Usually, there is a payment to be made by owners reclaiming their pet.

If you find a stray dog, contact your local authority as the Environmental Protection Act 1990 makes them legally responsible for taking in stray dogs.

Similarly, if your own dog has strayed, register the details with your local authority. Also check with animal sanctuaries, the police and veterinary surgeries. Look on websites such as those for animal charities; additionally, there are websites specifically dedicated to lost pets.

*Whenever puppies or dogs are abandoned, they must be reported to your local authority.*

## Dog collars and leads

It is a legal requirement for a dog when in a street to wear a collar bearing the owner's name and contact details – and to be on a lead.

## Worrying livestock

The law considers the worrying of livestock on agricultural land to be a serious offence. The owner of a dog which has been worrying livestock can be detained by a police officer and made liable for damages. A control order may be issued to the owner, or even an order for the dog's destruction.

Therefore, when taking your dog for a walk in the countryside where livestock are present, always keep your pet on a lead.

## Dog fouling

This is a serious offence as not only are dog faeces unsightly and dangerously slippery if stepped on, but they may contain worm eggs which can lead to toxocariasis, a serious infection in children that can result in loss of eyesight.

Local authorities have power under the Clean Neighbourhood and Environment Act 2005 to create 'dog control orders'; this bans dogs in certain areas, either completely or unless on a lead. Additionally, dog wardens have the power to initiate fines.

## Dangerous dogs

As a result of a spate of dogs attacking people during the latter decades of the 1900s, the Dangerous Dogs Act was enacted in 1991. It imposes severe restrictions on the ownership of Pit Bull Terriers, Japanese Tosas, Dogo Argentinos and Fila Brasileiros, breeds which initially were bred for aggression.

Regulations include compulsory insurance, neutering, tattooing and microchipping for such dogs, as well as their entry on the Index of Exempted Dogs. It is also a legal requirement to keep them on a muzzle and lead when in public places.

*Owners of some breeds, including Pit Bull Terriers, are legally obliged to register their ownership.*

### Road accidents

Should there be a road accident involving a dog, the driver must stop and the matter must be reported to the police within 24 hours. The owner of the dog causing the accident may be liable for damages.

Some pet insurances – apart from recompensing veterinary fees – encompass third-party cover for accidents.

If you find an animal which has been severely injured as a result of a traffic accident, immediately phone the police and report the matter. The police have the authority to call a vet to the scene to attend to the needs of the animal.

*Quarantine is not automatically required when a pet enters or leaves the British Isles (see below).*

## Pet passports

In 2000, radical changes were made to the existing and highly effective quarantine laws. It enabled dogs and cats with pet passports to travel from the UK to western Europe, and to return, if they had a current European Union pet passport.

A derogation that covered animals in rabies-free countries (United Kingdom, Ireland, Sweden and Malta), provided an interim period to allow these countries to formulate a rabies control strategy. However, the European Commission agreed to maintain precautions to keep the tapeworm *Echinococcus multilocularis* out of these countries, even after 2012.

From the start of 2012, pets from anywhere in the world can enter the United Kingdom without quarantine, provided they meet the rules of the European Union Scheme (criteria of entry depends from where the pet is coming). It is advisable, particularly if bringing in a pet from a non-EU listed country, to contact the AHVLA (Animal Health and Veterinary Laboratories Agency) for their requirements in relation to the country the pet is leaving.

When intending to travel abroad to any country with your pet, first contact the AHVLA for details of the requirements for the destination country.

● **Exit and entry for your pet** is only through registered ports and airports.

● **Microchipping is essential** and this must be undertaken before the animal is vaccinated.

● **Vaccination against rabies is essential** and the animal must be at least 12 weeks old. The vaccination documentation includes the animal's microchip number and age. Ask your vet for current details of initial vaccinations, together with legally required follow-up ones.

## Animal Welfare Act 2006

When considering introducing a dog into your family's life, remember that the Animal Welfare Act requires anyone responsible for a pet to do what is reasonable to meet its welfare needs. The penalty for failing to take good care of your pet could be prosecution.

Your puppy or dog has a legal right to expect you to:
• Provide an adequate and proper diet throughout its life, and to ensure there is continuous access to clean, fresh water.

• Ensure it has somewhere to live and to be housed with, or apart, from other animals, as required.

• Allow it to express its normal behaviour. Part of this require-ment is to ensure that the animal has sufficient space for all of its natural activities.

• Provide protection from pain, suffering, injury and disease.

The Welsh Assembly Government and the English Government have both produced Codes of Practice to help pet owners meet the requirements of the law.

The majority of puppy and dog owners automatically and without reservation provide their pets with these conditions. However, if you notice or hear about a pet being mistreated, immediately contact the police or an animal welfare society. We all have a duty of responsibility to animals.

*For most puppies, life is packed with playing, sleeping and eating – a utopian recipe for life.*

# Glossary

The range of terms and abbreviations used in the dog world is extensive. Some of these have specialist applications, while others are in everyday use and widely known. Whatever their derivation, they all help in the understanding and caring for puppies and dogs.

*A puppy exhibiting the exuberance of puppyhood.*

**Apple head**
Skull with a rounded top, such as in toy spaniels.

**Apron**
On long-coated dogs this refers to the longer hair below the neck and on the chest. It is also known as a 'frill' and often seen in Spitz-type breeds.

**Babbler**
A hound that barks even when not out hunting and being 'on the trail'.

**Beard**
Profuse, rather broad and bushy whiskers, especially on the chin and seen in the Griffon Bruxellois.

**Beefy**
Over-heavy and developed hindquarters.

**Belton**
Description of a coat's colour – the intermingling of coloured and white hairs. For example, the lemon- or blue-flecked colours seen on certain English Setters.

**Bitch**
Female dog.

**Blaze**
White stripe running up the centre of the face and between the eyes.

**Blocked**
Having a cube-like or square formation of the head.

**Bloom**
The sheen on a coat when in prime condition.

**Blue-merle**
Description of a coat's colour – blue and grey mixed with black.

**Brace**
Two dogs.

**Breeching**
Tan-coloured hair on the inside of the thighs. This is often seen in the Manchester Terrier.

**Brindle**
Description of a coat's colour – a fine, even mixture of black hairs combined with those of a lighter colour, usually grey, tan or brown.

**Brisket**
The part of the body in front of the chest and between the forelegs.

**Broken colour**
Description of a coat's colour – a self-colour (single colour) broken by another colour.

**Brush**
Bushy tail, heavy with hair.

**Cheeky**
Having cheeks that are rounded, or thick and protruding.

**Chiselled**
Having a clean-cut shape of head, particularly in the area beneath the eyes.

**Chops**
Jowls, or pendulous flesh on the lips and jaw, often seen in a Bulldog.

**Clipping**
Trimming the coat.

**Cloddy**
Low, thick-set and comparatively heavy.

**Cobby**
Short-bodied and compact.

**Corky**
Active, lively and alert.

**Cow-hocked**
When the hocks turn towards each other.

**Crest**
Upper arched part of the neck.

**Cropping**
Cutting and trimming of an ear so that it forms a point and stands erect. This practice is illegal in England and Wales, and in European countries that have ratified the European Convention for the Protection of Pet Animals.

**Cross-breed**
Dog that is the product of a sire and dam that are representatives of two different pure breeds.

**Croup**
Rear part of the back, above the hind legs.

**Crown**
Highest part of the head.

**Culotte**
Longer hair on the back of the thighs. Schipperkes usually have this characteristic.

**Cushion**
Fullness or thickness of the upper lips. Pekingese have this characteristic.

**Dam**
Female parent of puppies and generally applied to a bitch from the time of whelping (the act of giving birth) a litter to the weaning of her last puppy in that litter.

**Dappled**
Having mottled markings of different colours, with no one colour being dominant.

**Dead grass**
Refers to the colour of dull straw or tan. Also known as Sedge.

**Debarking**
Removing a dog's ability to bark. This practice is illegal in the British Isles.

**Dew-claws**
Rudimentary fifth digits and claws found on the inside of the legs below the hocks; they are usually removed at an early stage.

**Dewlap**
Loose and pendulous skin under the throat.

**Docking**
Earlier practice of shortening a tail. This is now illegal in the British Isles unless done by a vet for prophylactic reasons.

**Dog**
Male dog; also collectively used for both male and female animals.

**Dome**
Rounded skull of some dogs, particularly spaniels.

**Fall**
Loose and long hair overhanging the face. This can be seen in the Skye Terrier and Yorkshire Terrier.

**Feathering**
Longer hair on the ears, legs, tail or body.

**Felted**
When a coat has become matted.

**Flag**
Long, fine and silky hairs hanging under the tails of setters and some retrievers, graduating in length from long at the root to short at its tip.

**Flank**
Side of a dog's body between the last rib and hip.

**Flare**
Blaze that widens at its top.

**Forearm**
Bone of the foreleg between the elbow and the pastern.

**Foreface**
Front part of the head; before the eyes and sometimes known as the muzzle.

**Forelock**
Abundant tussle of hair growing on the forehead and falling forwards over the eyes, like a drooping peak of a cap. This characteristic can be seen in the Kerry Blue Terrier.

**Frill**
Another term for apron.

**Front**
Forepart of the body as seen head-on. This includes the forelegs, chest, brisket and shoulder line.

**Grizzle**
Bluish-grey or iron-grey colour.

**Gun-shy**
Describes a dog that fears the sound or sight of a gun.

**Hard-mouth**
Dog that bites and marks with his teeth the game he retrieves.

**Harlequin**
Patched or pied coloration, usually black-and-white.

**Heat**
Seasonal period of a bitch, which is said to be 'in heat', 'on heat' or 'in season'.

**Heel**
Another term for hock.

**Height**
Vertical measurement from the withers to the ground. Sometimes, this is referred to as shoulder height.

**Hock**
Tarsus or collection of bones of the hind leg, forming the joint between the second thigh and metatarsals.

**Hound**
Term commonly used for a dog that hunts by scent.

**Hound-marked**
When the colour conforms to the conventional patterning seen on hounds – a dark saddle (usually black),

dark ears and head (usually tan), and the rest of the dog white.

**Inbreeding**
Mating of closely related dogs within the same breed.

**Isabella**
Colour description – fawn or light bay.

**Kissing spots**
Attractive spots on the cheeks of some small breeds and especially the spot in the centre of the forehead of the Blenheim-type King Charles Spaniel.

**Lippy**
Having pendulous lips, or lips that do not fit tightly.

**Loins**
Region of the body on either side of the backbone and between the last ribs and the hindquarters.

**Lumbering**
Having an awkward gait.

**Maiden**
Unmated bitch.

**Mane**
Profuse hair growing on the upper side of the neck.

**Mantle**
Dark-shaded part of the coat, on the shoulders, back and sides. This feature is often seen on the Saint Bernard.

**Mask**
Dark shading on the foreface. This often occurs on breeds such as Mastiff, Boxer and Pekingese.

**Matron**
Bitch kept for breeding purposes, sometimes known as a brood bitch.

**Merle**
Term for a blue-grey colour mixture, flecked or ticked with black.

**Mongrel**
Dog of mixed origin, often formed from several breeds.

**Muzzle**
Head in front of the eyes.

**Muzzle-band**
White marking around the muzzle, often seen on the Boston Terrier.

**Nose**
Ability to detect and follow scents.

**Occiput**
Upper, back point of the skull. Also known as peak.

**Oestrum**
Menstrual cycle. A bitch experiences oestral periods approximately every six months. When this condition is present, the bitch is said to be 'on heat', 'in heat' or 'in season'; she is sexually excited and in the correct condition to be mated by a male dog.

**Otter tail**
Tail that is thick at its root, round and tapering, with the hair parted or divided on the underside.

**Overhang**
Heavy or pronounced brow. This is usually seen in the Pekingese.

**Overshot**
When the front teeth of the upper jaw overlap the front teeth of the lower jaw when the mouth is closed.

**Paddling**
Moving with the forefeet wide apart; this results in a roll or swing of the body.

**Pads**
Tough, shock-absorbing projections on the undersides of feet. They are sometimes known as soles.

**Parti-coloured**
Variegated, in patches of two or more colours in approximately equal proportions.

**Pastern**
Lowest part of the leg – below the knee on the foreleg or below the hock on the hind leg.

**Peak**
Upper, back point of the skull. Also known as occiput.

**Pied**
Comparatively large patches of two or more colours, in unequal proportions.

**Pile**
Dense undercoat of soft hair.

**Plume**
Feathered tail carried arched over the back.

**Pompon**
Rounded tuft of hair left on the end of a tail when the coat is clipped. This is often seen on a Poodle.

**Prick-eared**
With the ears carried erect and usually pointed at the tip, as in the German Shepherd Dog and Welsh Corgi.

**Ring-tailed**
With the tail carried up and around, almost in a circle.

**Roan**
Fine mixture of coloured and white hairs. These are seen in colour medleys such as 'blue-roan', 'orange-roan' and 'lemon-roan'.

**Roman nose**
Nose with a comparatively high bridge that forms a slightly convex line from the forehead to the tip of the nose.

**Ruff**
Thick, long hair around the neck.

**Sable**
Lacing of black hairs in, or over, a lighter base colour.

**Saddle**
Black marking over the back, resembling a saddle.

**Screw tail**
Naturally short tail twisted in more or less a spiral.

**Sedge**
Refers to the colour of dull straw or tan. Also known as dead grass.

**Service**
Act of copulation, when a bitch is mated by a dog.

**Sickle tail**
Tail carried in a semicircle.

**Sire**
Male parent of a litter of puppies.

**Snipey**
Having a pointed, weak muzzle.

**Snowshoe foot**
Foot that has slight webbing between the toes.

**Soft-mouth**
Dog that can retrieve an object without damaging it. The term has special reference to gundogs, who are trained to retrieve game without causing damage.

**Spayed**
Describes a female whose ovaries have been removed surgically.

**Spectacles**
Shading or dark markings over or around the eyes.

**Splashed**
With irregular colour patches, such as a colour on white, or white on a colour.

**Squirrel tail**
Tail carried upwards and curving more or less forward.

**Stance**
Manner of standing.

**Staring coat**
Hair when dry – harsh and sometimes curling at its tips.

**Stern**
Often used to refer to the tail area of a dog.

**Stifle**
Joint on the hind leg between the first thigh and the second thigh. It is analogous to the knee in man.

**Stud dog**
Male dog kept solely or partly for breeding purposes.

**Temple**
Area behind the eyes and below the ears.

**Thigh**
Top section of the hind legs – the hindquarters.

**Ticked**
Having comparatively small, isolated areas of black or coloured hairs on a white background.

**Tie**
Term used in reference to a dog and bitch locked together after copulation. During ejaculation, the bulbous base of the penis swells within the vagina and causes a 'tie' between them, usually lasting 10–15 minutes.

**Topknot**
Tuft of hair on the top of the head. This is often seen on the Bedlington Terrier, Dandie Dinmont Terrier and Irish Water Spaniel.

**Trace**
Dark line which runs down the back of a Pug.

**Tri-coloured**
Indicates three colours on a dog when they appear more or less in the same proportion.

**Trousers**
Hair on the hindquarters of a dog, especially seen on the Afghan Hound.

**Tucked-up**
Describes the loins of a dog when lifted well up, such as with the Borzoi, Greyhound and Whippet.

**Turn-up**
Uptilted jaw, as seen in a Bulldog.

**Type**
Characteristics that distinguish a breed.

**Undershot**
When the front teeth of the lower jaw overlap or project beyond the front teeth of the upper jaw when the mouth is closed.

**Vent**
In general terms, the area around the anus. However, it often refers to the tan-coloured hair underneath the tail of some breeds, such as the Manchester Terrier.

**Wheaten**
Pale yellow or fawn colour.

**Whelping**
Act of giving birth to puppies.

**Whelps**
Newly born puppies.

**Whip tail**
Tail carried stiff and straight.

**Whole colour**
Colour which covers the whole body.

**Wire-haired**
Describes a coat that is hard, crisp and wiry in texture.

**Withers**
Highest part of the body, just behind the neck.

**Wrinkle**
Loose, folded skin on the forehead or foreface.

*Collies are frequently claimed to be the most intelligent breed.*

# Index

**Acknowledgments**

Fine Folio Publishing would like to thank the following for kindly providing pictures of breeds:

Norwegian Elkhound: Copyright © Mrs. Linda Middleton,
photograph by Alan Walker, www.alanvwalker.co.uk

Cardiganshire Welsh Corgi: Mary Bloom, http://marybloom.com

Affenpinscher, Irish Water Spaniel and Welsh Springer Spaniel:
Michael Trafford, www.traffordphotos.com

Additional photographs: Fotolia and iStockphoto.